New York–Paris

New York–Paris

Whitman, Baudelaire, AND THE Hybrid City

Laure Katsaros

THE UNIVERSITY OF MICHIGAN PRESS ANN ARBOR

For George, Pierre, & Elias

Copyright © by the University of Michigan 2012
All rights reserved

Published in the United States of America by
The University of Michigan Press
Manufactured in the United States of America
♾ Printed on acid-free paper

2015   2014   2013   2012   4   3   2   1

A CIP catalog record for this book is available from the British Library.

Library of Congress Cataloging-in-Publication Data

Katsaros, Laure.
    New York–Paris : Whitman, Baudelaire, and the hybrid city / Laure Katsaros.
        p.   cm.
    Includes bibliographical references and index.
    ISBN 978-0-472-11849-6 (cloth : acid-free paper) — ISBN 978-0-472-02870-2 (e-book)
    1. Whitman, Walt, 1819–1892—Criticism and interpretation.
2. Baudelaire, Charles, 1821–1867—Criticism and interpretation.   3. New York (N.Y.)—In literature.   4. Paris (France)—In literature.   5. Comparative literature—American and French.   6. Comparative literature—French and American.   I. Title.
PS3233.K38   2012
811'.3—dc23   2012019744

Contents

Introduction
1

ONE
A Call in the
Midst of the Crowd
13

TWO
This Insubstantial Pageant
34

THREE
A Portrait of the Artist
as Parisian Prowler
55

FOUR
Dark Rooms
80

Conclusion
99

Notes   *Bibliography*   *Index*
111   133   143

Introduction

To write *one hundred* of these belabored nothings, I have
to be in a constant state of elation . . . and I also need the
strange intoxication of spectacles, crowds, music, even
streetlights!
    —Charles Baudelaire, letter to Sainte-Beuve, May 4, 1865

New-York loves crowds—and I do, too. I can no more get
along without houses, civilization, aggregations of humanity,
meetings, hotels, theatres, than I can get along without food.
            —Walt Whitman, *New York Tribune,* August 1881

IN NINETEENTH-CENTURY STEREOSCOPES, two nearly identical images are printed side by side on a strip. If you look at them intently, a
third, three-dimensional image emerges. But what happens when New
York and Paris, Whitman and Baudelaire, are placed side by side? These
two celebrated faces of the modern city seem to have almost nothing in
common. In 1983, the Baudelaire scholar W. T. Bandy remarked that trying to find points of resemblance between Walt Whitman and Charles
Baudelaire reminded him of a riddle about the American presidency:
"Why are Calvin Coolidge and Ulysses S. Grant alike? Both had thick
black beards . . . except Calvin Coolidge."[1] Placing Whitman and Baudelaire on the same stereoscopic strip is unnatural, as if the two portraits
could never merge into one, and the third image were not three-dimensional, but the equivalent of seeing Whitman's long white beard superimposed on Baudelaire's clean-shaven face. What seems to appear is not
a likeness of them both, but a ludicrous pastiche—a mustache on the

Mona Lisa. It has been almost impossible, ever since the middle of the nineteenth century, to see Whitman and Baudelaire in the same frame.

Though their life spans overlapped, their paths never crossed. Except for a brief period in New Orleans, Whitman lived in Brooklyn and New York (as Manhattan was then called) until the Civil War. Baudelaire never visited America, and left Paris only under duress. They did not translate each other's work, did not enter into a correspondence, and had no common friends. They showed almost no sign of being aware of the other's existence. Baudelaire, who made celebrated translations of Longfellow and Poe, knew English well, but no reference to Whitman can be found in anything he wrote. Whitman, who read French writers in English translation only, alludes to Baudelaire just once. In an essay entitled "Poetry of the Future," Whitman refers to Baudelaire's article "The Pagan School," which speaks of the corrosive consequences of an excessive love of beauty. "'The immoderate taste for beauty and art,' says Charles Baudelaire," in the quotation by Whitman, "'leads men into monstrous excesses. In minds imbued with a frantic greed for the beautiful, all the balances of justice and truth disappear. There is a lust, a disease of the art faculties, which eats up the moral like a cancer.'"[2] Adducing this argument as evidence that the hypertrophy of the aesthetic sense will inevitably erode the moral faculties, Whitman uses Baudelaire to justify his own belief that poetry must sing of real life and ordinary days, and not the hyperbolically "poetic" subjects that it had always been accustomed to invoking. The fact that Whitman saw Charles Baudelaire as the proponent of morality, moderation, and restraint reveals a profound misunderstanding of his contemporary.

The first edition of *Leaves of Grass* appeared in 1855, and until Whitman's death, was endlessly revised. Shortly after its first appearance, an anonymous English critic, alleging that Whitman's long lines had drifted from the regular rhythms of verse into the slack shapelessness of prose, claimed that "Whitman was as unacquainted with poetry as a hog with mathematics."[3] Baudelaire's first two prose poems, "Evening Twilight" and "Solitude," also appeared in 1855. More prose poems were published in a scattering of Parisian literary journals during the following decade. They were unenthusiastically received by such critics as Gustave Bourdin from *Le Figaro,* who diagnosed them as the symptoms of the "dark and sick soul" of a "sullen flaneur."[4] If the reactions of their first critics are to be trusted, Whitman and Baudelaire were disliked for opposite reasons. Whitman lacked artfulness and grace, while Baudelaire carried the refinement of his art to the point of morbid excess, even when he crossed over the boundary into the starkest prose. While Whitman exhibited a shocking lack of self-awareness, Baudelaire appeared pathologically self-conscious. One too primitive, the other too decadent, they seemed to come from opposite ends of time.

In 1926, T. S. Eliot wondered whether "any age" other than the nineteenth century could "have produced more heterogeneous" figures than Whitman and Baudelaire, explaining that, for Whitman, "there was no chasm between the real and the ideal, such as opened before the horrified eyes of Baudelaire."[5] Baudelaire saw the world caught in a hopeless struggle between an all-pervasive squalor and rare sparks of grace, whereas Whitman has been considered not only as the representative of a stereotypically American optimism, but also as someone who could find beauty even in the lowest and most common of spectacles. Baudelaire's irony creates an extraordinary distance between what he says and what he appears to mean. In contrast, it is easy to believe that a transparently candid Whitman exposes every aspect of himself in *Leaves of Grass*. Whitman seems to invite us to take him at his word; Baudelaire urges us to never trust what he says, or what he seems to have said, if only we could have pinned down his meaning.

The aesthetic differences between Whitman and Baudelaire are often seen as the offshoot of their opposing political views. On the rare occasions when they are compared, we inevitably find them at extreme and opposite ends of the political spectrum.[6] Walter Whitman Jr., who simplified—one could even say "democratized"—his first name into "Walt," has mythologized himself, and has been mythologized ever after, as an innocent and heroic exemplar of American democracy. From the highest to the lowest, everything finds its place and stands on equal footing inside his poems. Baudelaire's life, in contrast, was increasingly consumed by a bitter hostility to progress, to capitalism, and to America. In an essay on Edgar Allan Poe, Baudelaire denounced the United States as "a gigantic and childish country" whose commercial growth was "abnormal, even monstrous," and ridiculed its "naive faith in the omnipotence of industry."[7] He who had never traveled to America coined the derisive verb *américaniser* ("to Americanize"), which would ever after become the rhetorical high point of countless anti-American diatribes in France. Baudelaire even prophesied that the approaching decadence of Europe would coincide with "the domination of America and of industry."[8] It was as if the decline of one were indissolubly linked to the rise of the other—the New World and the Old constantly at war with one another. From Baudelaire's perspective, America's gain would inevitably be France's loss.

Whitman, however, looked on France in a completely different light than Baudelaire looked on America. Although he grew up in Brooklyn, Whitman went so far as to claim the status of "a real Parisian" in a poem with a French title, "Salut au Monde." Yet all that Whitman found most luminous about France was precisely what Baudelaire most abhorred. As Roger Asselineau has shown, Whitman pictured France as the capital of democracy in Old Europe and admired the revolutionary spirit of 1789 and 1848.[9] In "Salut au Monde," he praises the French for their "fierce liberty songs," while in a poem written in memory of the Terror of 1794, he addresses Democracy, in democracy's own language, as "ma femme." He even composes his own revolutionary song for France, the home of his imaginary bride: "I send these words to Paris with my love / And I guess some chansonniers there will understand them."[10] In another poem addressed to the French nation, this time after its humiliating defeat in the Franco-Prussian War of 1870, Whitman refers to France as a "frivolous, mocking land," but also as a "heroic" one, where the star of liberty will be reborn. He was enraptured by Victor Hugo, the Romantic historian Jules Michelet, and George Sand. For Whitman, Sand was "the brightest woman ever born."[11] In private, Baudelaire called Sand a "fat cow" and a "stupid creature"; she reminded him, he claimed, of a latrine.[12] In the eyes of Baudelaire, a writer like Sand, who extolled the virtues of the disenfranchised, wrote sentimental prose about the poor, and defended the rights of women, was a symptom of the irreversible decline of French culture. But the woman that Baudelaire likened to a latrine represented a political and literary ideal for Whitman.

In one of Baudelaire's prose poems, an abominably ugly man looks at himself in the mirror. When asked why he has chosen to inflict such a spectacle on himself, the man answers that "in the name of the immortal principles of 1789" (namely, that all men are equal before the eyes of the law), no one can deny him the right to look at his own image. For Baudelaire, the egalitarian ideals of postrevolutionary France had a catastrophic effect on aesthetic values, and the poem is a thinly veiled allegory of the modern era. As usefulness became a more precious treasure than beauty, the inevitable consequence was that the public, instead of being horrified by ugliness, turned a blind eye to it. From Baudelaire's perspective, nineteenth-century France saw the collapse of the social and cultural system that had allowed the creation of art. But all of Whitman's poetry gives voice to the opposite belief. Every form of life, no matter how low, base, or degraded, is considered sacred in *Leaves of Grass*. Beauty is an aristocratic concept for Baudelaire, while Whitman's idea of the beautiful is inherently democratic: the purpose of poetry, for him, is to sanctify the egalitarian ideals of democracy.

Baudelaire and Whitman arrived at their views of modernity from radically opposed directions. One, seemingly, by clinging to the past, became acutely aware of each and every sign foretelling the advent of a future world, while the other, by turning away from the past, deliberately chose to face the future head-on. Like the New York he has come to epitomize, Whitman stands at the beginning of a new era. Baudelaire, the self-declared enemy of progress, stands in a Paris that was on the cusp of ceasing to be itself. Walter Benjamin could not resist framing his analysis of the two poets and the cities they stood for as a dichotomy between optimism and nostalgia:

> Baudelaire's opposition to progress was the indispensable condition for his success in capturing Paris in his poetry. Compared with this poetry, all later big-city lyric must be accounted feeble.
>
> What it lacks is precisely that reserve toward its subject matter which Baudelaire owed to his frenetic hatred of progress.
>
> *But what of Walt Whitman?*[13]

In this view, Baudelaire is the voice of the cynicism, pessimism, and waning energy of the Old World—an embodiment of the dismal realization that the future only repeats the past, and that, as a consequence, any course of action is in vain. By contrast, Whitman's poetry of New York would represent a young nation as it struggles, successfully, to create its own identity. Whitman heralds the irresistible progress that transformed America into the Goliath it became, while Baudelaire foreshadows the decline both of the Old World and of Paris, its artistic capital in the nineteenth century.

Just as their native cities epitomize either the Old World or the New, Whitman and Baudelaire have become iconic figures of nineteenth-century poetry. The claim, endlessly publicized by Whitman himself, that *Leaves of Grass* marked the true beginnings of American poetry has taken hold. Baudelaire, who in his own time was forced to make a name for himself in the wake of an infamous generation of French Romantics, has now eclipsed the poets who came before him to such an extent that their work has come to seem hopelessly dated. In retrospect, Baudelaire is widely credited with having invented our sense of the modern. His cynicism, irony, and desperation have refused to age, while the ideals of the Romantic generation, from a contemporary perspective, seem antediluvian. Because the lives of Baudelaire and Whitman coincided with the

Étienne Carjat,
*Portrait of Charles
Baudelaire*, 1863.
Bibliothèque
Nationale de
France, Paris

G. Frank Pearsall, portrait
of Walt Whitman, 1872.
Rare Books Division, The
New York Public Library,
Astor, Lenox and Tilden
Foundations

beginnings of photography, their likenesses have become indelible and opposing images of what a poet looks like. Charles Baudelaire's disconcerting appearance was immortalized by Étienne Carjat and by Nadar, the torment all too visible in his clean-shaven face.

Nicknamed "Monseigneur Brummel" by his friends, after Beau Brummel, the celebrated British dandy, Baudelaire as a young man would sometimes wear a blood-red cravat, pink gloves, and a purple boa, according to his friend Nadar.[14] Cursed throughout his brief existence by pride, poverty, solitude, and catastrophic physical decline, Baudelaire's life has ever after become a gold standard of the *poète maudit*. Walt Whitman, on the other hand, has left an image equally iconic, and yet utterly opposed to Baudelaire's. With his white beard and clear blue eyes, no torment is visible. There is only the masked repose of a face invisible behind the flowing white beard of an old man (and yet Whitman was only 53 when the photograph was taken).

Whitman's image, lacking Baudelaire's uncannily visible despair, has had a nearly immortal life of its own: it has been used to sell coffee, cigars, whiskey, and insurance. His likeness has appeared on matchbooks and postcards, and his apparently benevolent words, as the verbal equivalent of his image, are inscribed in public places.[15]

But from the perspective the nineteenth century, Baudelaire and Whitman had this much in common: they horrified their contemporaries by dragging poetry from the ethereal regions of Parnassus and into the squalor of the cities where they lived. Both *Leaves of Grass* and *Les Fleurs du mal* attracted the unwanted attention of censors. Baudelaire was famously put on trial by the French government in 1857 for "offense to public and religious morals." He was sentenced to pay a heavy fine and to excise some of the more scandalous poems from the collection. Baudelaire himself was well aware of the shock some of his poems could cause: as he wryly noted, "This book has not been written for my wives, my daughters, or my sisters; nor for anyone else's."[16] Although he was never subjected to the indignity of a public trial, Whitman scandalized the literary and political establishment throughout his life. In 1860, Ralph Waldo Emerson urged him to drop a poem entitled "To a Common Prostitute" from the forthcoming edition of *Leaves of Grass* (Whitman refused). Before the sixth edition went to press in 1881, the publisher, James Osgood, having been warned that the book violated obscenity laws, again proposed to remove "To a Common Prostitute" (Whitman found another publisher).[17]

Both Whitman and Baudelaire, in the eyes of their more conventional contemporaries, degraded artistic and moral ideals by speaking of outcasts and ordinary people in a language more direct than poetry had ever used before. Baudelaire rejected the narrow definition of "realism" as a mere imitation of reality. He famously said of his hero, the Romantic painter Eugène Delacroix, that a true artist should "illuminate reality" and "project its reflection onto other people's minds" instead of merely duplicating it.[18] Yet if realism is defined as the incorporation of details taken from real life into art, Baudelaire's poetry must be labeled realistic. Even as he derided the self-proclaimed realism of his friends the painter Gustave Courbet and the writer Champfleury, Baudelaire declared, "There has never been a good poet who was not a *realist*."[19]

Whitman, too, can be called a realist in the sense that he brought almost every aspect of life in America into his poetry. In his notebooks, he reminded himself to put into his poems "*American things, idioms, materials, persons, groups, minerals, vegetables, animals, etc.*"[20] Even Ezra Pound, despite his early antipathy, observed in 1934 that one could "learn more of nineteenth-century America from Whitman than from any of the writers who either refrained from perceiving, or limited their record to what they had been taught to consider suitable literary expression."[21] Similarly, Baudelaire argued in an essay entitled "On the Heroism of Modern Life" that, despite the opinions of those who lamented the disappearance of classical models of art, the contemporary frock coat was as sublime as the toga. "Parisian life," he noted, "is rich in poetic and wonderful subjects. . . . The marvelous is all around us and permeates us; but we do not see it."[22] In the opening lines of "Passage to India," Whitman dreams not of wearing a toga, but of being the Homer of modern times, singing "the great achievements of the present" and its "modern wonders." To believe that the present contained as many wonders as the past, and that it could be a richer source of poetic invention, brought Whitman and Baudelaire far closer together than Eliot could have imagined.

In Whitman's lifetime, the two poets were often linked as representatives of a radical new trend in poetry. The Symbolist poet Jules Laforgue introduced Whitman to the literary avant-garde of late nineteenth-century Paris. In 1886, he published translations of the poems "Inscriptions," "O Star of France," and "A Woman Waits for Me." Before his premature death from tuberculosis, he was planning the first complete French translation of *Leaves of Grass*. He was also the first to note that both Whitman and Baudelaire pioneered the use of an ordinary language, rather than an elevated or self-consciously "poetic" diction.[23]

Laforgue even argued that Baudelaire's purposefully crude and prosaic metaphors were evidence of nothing less than his "Americanism," as if the terms "crude," "prosaic," "unpoetic," and "American" were interchangeable. Conversely, an American reviewer of "Charles Pierre Baudelaire," in 1871, linked Baudelaire with Whitman under the term "realism," observing that realism "is the distinguishing characteristic of the highest literature of the day, and finds its broadest expression with us in the writings of Walt Whitman."[24] Another American reviewer, in 1869, noted that Baudelaire's poems "have the same masculine and refreshingly frank character that we find in the less musical utterances of Walt Whitman," adding that "the resemblance is entirely due to the uniformity of the genuine, virile, poetic mind . . . which is opposed to perfumed drawing-room daintiness."[25]

From the perspective of the nineteenth century, both Baudelaire and Whitman fell under the aegis of realism. Unlike their predecessors, who were apparently content with the interior world of "perfumed drawing-room daintiness," they opened the doors to the world outside. But what they immersed themselves in was not the peace of the countryside, or the wildness of the mountains and seashore. What they freely entered in and became obsessed by were the crowds that streamed through nineteenth-century streets. Life in the teeming cities was an irreducible and essential aspect not only of their daily lives, but also of their poetry. Walter Benjamin claimed that, with Baudelaire, Paris became "for the first time the subject of lyric poetry."[26] Forty years earlier, William James had written that Whitman "felt the human crowd as rapturously as Wordsworth felt the mountains." Both Whitman and Baudelaire were fascinated witnesses to the tableaux of mid-nineteenth-century street life, and they recorded what they witnessed not only in prose, essays, or letters, but in their poems. From the perspective of the nineteenth century, they embodied a paradox: how can one drag the prose of the city into the ideal world of poetry, without transforming a poetic world into a prosaic one? How can a subject that is irredeemably unpoetic become part of a poem without denaturing poetry itself? No poet before them had ever tried, and so the act of bringing such unpoetic scenes into the world of poetry came as a shock to their contemporaries. But from the perspective of our time, the shock has come to seem inexplicable. What could be a more fitting subject for modern poetry than the after-effects of living in a city? If we see nothing out of the ordinary in this act, it is because Baudelaire and Whitman have accustomed us to it. They have turned our gaze from the individual to the crowds; and they have led us from the interiority of closed rooms and individual selves to the outside world of crowded agglomerations and borderless spaces.

Baudelaire's poetry is in the deepest sense an offshoot of his life in Paris, just as Whitman's is an offshoot of New York. In both cases their experience, refracted through their poetry, was of a key moment in the lives of their respective cities. New York and Paris were profoundly transformed in the second half of the nineteenth century. Much of what was distinctive about each city was destroyed and reconfigured. Whitman and Baudelaire were witnesses to cities that were suddenly emerging from the chrysalis of their former selves. In the middle of the nineteenth century, New York was in a state of radical flux. In 1856, a journalist went so far as to lament that the city was "never the same for a dozen years together." The effect of this transmutation was profoundly disorienting, so much so that "A man born in New York forty years ago finds nothing, absolutely nothing of the New York he knew."[27] Mid-nineteenth-century Paris was no less radically transformed. Under the supervision of Haussmann, age-old accretions of convoluted streets and elaborate stone hovels were razed to the ground so as to make way for wide new boulevards and long rows of symmetrical buildings. The transformation was merciless. Even the most hallowed vestiges of the past were not spared. In a profoundly American gesture, Haussmann had planned to relocate the most celebrated of Parisian cemeteries, the Père-Lachaise, to the suburbs outside Paris. A decade after the start of the transformation, in 1867, the anti-Haussmann pamphleteer Louis Veuillot predicted that in the new Paris, "there will be no more houses, no more tombstones, no more graveyards even." Veuillot's dirge for the Old Paris found a resonance among those who, across the Atlantic, deplored the transformation of the New York cityscape. In 1845, a former mayor of New York lamented that "the very bones of our ancestors are not permitted to lie quiet a quarter of a century, and one generation of men seems studious to remove all relics of those who precede them."[28] In mid-nineteenth-century Paris and New York, the past, suddenly, was no longer held in reverence. Even aesthetic forms were discarded, and replaced with structures that were radically new. Whitman wrote long lines of verse that looked, and sounded, like prose. After proposing brilliant variations on traditional forms, Baudelaire devoted the last years of his poetic life to prose poetry.

The image of Baudelaire's Paris began to crystallize in the "Parisian

Scenes" (*Tableaux parisiens*) within the verse poems of *The Flowers of Evil* (*Les Fleurs du mal*), and then finalized itself in a series of fifty prose poems written between the early 1850s and the mid-1860s. The collection was variously entitled *Poems of the Night* (*Poèmes nocturnes*), *The Solitary Wanderer* (*Le promeneur solitaire*), *The Parisian Prowler* (*Le rôdeur parisien*), and *Glimmer and Smoke* (*La lueur et la fumée*), until Baudelaire settled on the dual title *Le Spleen de Paris* and *Petits poèmes en prose*. Though not all the poems are set in contemporary Paris, Baudelaire's *Petits poèmes en prose* capture a quintessentially Parisian world of crowded funfairs, boulevards, public gardens, brothels, cabarets, and bleak faubourgs. *Le Spleen de Paris* is unfinished. Like Whitman's perpetually edited and expanded *Leaves of Grass,* and unlike the epics of Virgil or Dante, it has no clear structure other than one of endless accretion. A moving image of the chaotic landscapes of their respective cities, *Leaves of Grass* and *Le Spleen de Paris* stand at a crucial intersection in time, when old structures were being obliterated and new ones were rising in their place.

Whitman's New York and the Paris of Baudelaire encapsulated the political, cultural, and aesthetic uncertainties of their times. All the evils Baudelaire associated with nineteenth-century France seemed to be concentrated in Paris. Whitman's vision of American democracy was inspired by his life in New York. For him, New York represented a microcosmic reflection of the United States; in the eyes of Baudelaire, Paris was just as closely identified with the rest of France. In one of Baudelaire's prose poems, an elegant Parisian reveler takes his hat off his hat to a donkey and wishes it a happy New Year. The reveler is then denounced as an incarnation of "the French spirit," which meant, in Baudelaire's eyes, the spirit of moral emptiness at the heart of a grossly materialistic culture.[29] Ironically, the Paris of Baudelaire is not a cosmopolitan city. In Baudelaire's prose poems, the intellectual capital of France and of nineteenth-century Europe appears as a cultural wasteland. It is the province of broken dreams, ruined ambitions, and philistines who are blind to any form of art. In 1860, Baudelaire wrote that "France is being overwhelmed by a base vulgarity," and that Paris itself was the "radiating center of universal stupidity."[30] Whitman's New York is the opposite; in his eyes at least, it is an extraordinarily cosmopolitan "City of the world," where no less than "All the lands of the earth make contributions."[31] It is as if New York and Paris had exchanged their auras. In Whitman's eyes, a city often identified not only with capitalism, but with ruthless robber-baronism, is transfigured into the cultural beacon of America, while in

Baudelaire's prose poems, Paris becomes synonymous with degradation, and is stigmatized as the most whorishly commercial of cities.

In *Leaves of Grass,* Whitman reinvents New York in the likeness of a European capital, while in *Le Spleen de Paris,* Baudelaire imagines the eponymous city as a copy of the American metropolis. The Paris of Baudelaire is not simply Paris; it is, instead, the urban hybrid that Baudelaire referred to in a letter to Victor Hugo as "our Paris—New York."[32] Forced by Napoleon III and Baron Haussmann to adopt the ideology of progress, and to project itself into a ruthlessly commercial future, Paris, in the eyes of Baudelaire, was being destroyed as it rushed headlong into its own future. Baudelaire is haunted by the chilling realization that the old Paris will inevitably vanish as it hurtles toward a future that is synonymous with Americanization. The city's past, in Baudelaire's estimation, will only be preserved as a relic or a corpse, with one of these relics being the poet Charles Baudelaire himself. Although Whitman, unlike Baudelaire, appears to embrace the future, his New York is no less haunted by the shadow of death, and by the memory of a native past that has been irretrievably lost. Whitman and Baudelaire projected an image of each city onto the other. For Whitman, Paris was what New York could and should become, while for Baudelaire, New York was an image of that which he feared Paris was becoming. In brief, Whitman's dream was that New York could become the Paris of the New World, while Baudelaire's nightmare was that Paris would become the New York of the Old World. What follows is an examination of these crossing echoes.

ONE

A Call in the
Midst of the Crowd

From Rowdy to Bartleby

IN NOVEMBER 1861, the first article on Whitman to appear in France was published in the Parisian literary journal *La Revue européenne*. The article was entitled "Walt Whitman, poëte, philosophe et 'rowdy.'" Baudelaire's poem "Recollection" (*Recueillement*) appeared in the same issue of the journal. It is impossible to imagine that Baudelaire, who went to extraordinary lengths to make sure that each of his published poems appeared exactly as he wanted them, did not take some interest in this American poet, philosopher, and "rowdy." But the impression of Walt Whitman he would have received is a distinctly repugnant one. The author of the article, a conservative critic named Louis Étienne, concluded that Whitman was a lawless and immoral charlatan—a worshipper of brute force and an apologist for homosexual love.[1] Denouncing *Leaves of Grass* as a "triumph of confusion, a religion of chaos and an apotheosis of disorder," Étienne ridiculed Whitman for his chameleon-like identity and panoply of voices: "He is the carpenter in the wilderness and the poet of the city, the adventurer in California and the bourgeois in New York . . . the friend of Methodist missionaries and the flaneur on Broadway . . . with his arms around two of his fellow 'rowdies.'"[2] Taking Whitman at his own word, the French critic blamed what he perceived to be Whitman's aesthetic failure on the American's irrational desire to be too many things at the same time. Even the title of the article points to the absurdity of combining in one person a poet, a philosopher, and a "rowdy" (in English). Étienne explained to his readers that an American rowdy was "a loudmouth and a troublemaker" (*un homme de tapage et de*

13

désordre). But to anyone living in New York, the word "rowdy" had a far more specific meaning, and even more pejorative connotations. Like "roughs" and "loafers," "rowdies" were gang members and petty criminals who made a living from stealing and had a reputation for extreme violence.[3]

Whitman himself was partly to blame for the fact that he was perceived by many of his contemporaries as a loud, vulgar, and violent New Yorker. Steadfastly refusing to be identified as a man of letters, he cultivated his image as a man of the streets—*un homme de tapage et de désordre*. In a self-written review published anonymously in the *Brooklyn Daily Times* in 1856, he claimed to be "a man who does not associate with literary people," but who "loves the streets—loves the docks—loves the free rasping talk of men."[4] Deriding the existing rogues' gallery of American poets as "a few little silly fans languidly moved by shrunken fingers," Whitman, who had boasted in the first three versions of "Song of Myself" that he was "an American, one of the roughs, a kosmos," set out to break the withered fingers and fragile fans of his effeminate contemporaries.[5] Although he complained in a letter to a friend that "personally the author of Leaves of Grass is in no sense or sort whatever the 'rough,' the 'eccentric,' 'vagabond' or queer person that the commentators . . . persist in making him,"[6] his posture as the embodiment of plebeian virility, exaggerated to the point of self-parody, was the weapon he used to take the world of letters by force.

Whitman has long been blamed for being excessive in everything—at once too raw and too ambitious, too barbaric and too histrionic, too sensual and too spiritual. His unwillingness to discriminate or to reject, his resistance to order, and his lack of measure have been perceived as incompatible with the classical notion of poetry as a patient, selective, and methodical craft. His choice of topics was considered scandalous, but his treatment of them shocked just as much. Taking an interest in the lives of whores, opium addicts, and roughs was bad enough. Describing such subjects in a neutral, matter-of-fact way instead of turning them into allegories of despair was a radical novelty. What made things even worse, however, was the obvious fact that Whitman's verse was as lawless as his subjects. Baudelaire also shocked his contemporaries with his depictions of the most sordid aspects of city life. But the polished and distant perfection of his verse in *Les Fleurs du mal* stands in deliberate contrast with the prosaic subjects of the poems, creating a rich dissonance between form and content. Algernon Charles Swinburne, a lifelong admirer and occasional correspondent of Baudelaire, wrote in defense of the controversial French poet that "The pervading note of spiritual tragedy . . . dignifies and justifies at all points his treatment of the darkest and strangest subjects."[7] In his review of the second, expurgated edition of *Les Fleurs du mal,* Swinburne effusively praised Baudelaire for his "perfect workmanship" and his uncanny ability "always to use the right word and the right rhyme."[8] Swinburne denounced Whitman, on the other hand, in terms that Louis Étienne would not have disavowed. In a vitriolic article which appeared in 1887, Swinburne repudiated his youthful enthusiasm for Whitman, basing his indictment less on the contents of *Leaves of Grass* than on the style. Comparing Whitman with the "muck-racking" Zola and the "terrorist" Communards of Paris, Swinburne vilified him for his "voluminous and incoherent effusions," "exuberant incontinence," and "feverish and convulsive style of writing." The essay ended with the suggestion that Whitman could perhaps raise himself to the level of a mediocre poet if he decided to "resign all claim to the laurels of Gotham with which the critical sages of that famous borough have bedecked his unbashful brows."[9]

In Étienne's article as in Swinburne's change of heart, Whitman's identification with New York becomes a weapon in the hands of his detractors. The word "Gotham" is uttered with contempt, as if New York were self-evidently the most barbaric city on earth. By the second half of the nineteenth century, this attitude was pervasive. New York impressed many in Europe as a brutal and chaotic city, which cared only for the future and had no respect for the past. The elites of London and Paris perceived New York as an inferno of commerce and a cultural wasteland. In Stendhal's *The Charterhouse of Parma,* Count Mosca discourages the young hero Fabrice from emigrating to New York with these words: "In America, in the Republic, you get bored paying court to shopkeepers all day, and you become as stupid as they are; even worse, there is no Opera."[10] Like all jokes, Stendhal's is unfair. Opera houses did exist in America. Whitman was often seen at the Park Theater, the Astor Place Opera House, and the Bowery Theater in New York; and he loved Italian opera as much as Count Mosca did.[11] "But for the opera I could not have written *Leaves of Grass*," he confessed to a friend.[12] Whitman even revered the same actor as Baudelaire, William Macready, the English tragedian whose rivalry with and alleged contempt for the American actor Edwin Forrest incensed the nationalistic New York "rowdies" to such an extent that they caused the Astor Place Theater riot of May 1849.[13] The bloodthirsty rowdies who fought with the police and militia as they tried to force their way into the Astor Place Theater House clearly had their own opinion on the best way to play Shakespeare. Mid-nineteenth-century New York could even boast that it had its own artistic "Bohemia," a circle led by the journalist and theatrical critic Henry J. Clapp, to which Whitman adhered in the late 1850s. The New World Bohemians gathered every night in the basement of Pfaff's Restaurant on Broadway, just north of Bleecker Street, in the heart of the city's busiest shopping district.[14] But the New York Bohemia was a very distant relation of its Parisian avatar. "Far from a pack of free-and-easy artistic vagabonds," the crowd at Pfaff's was essentially composed of "hard-working writers who made penurious livings from the penny press and magazines."[15] It was impossible to escape the harsh commercial reality of life in New York, and to make a living from literature alone. Mid-nineteenth-century New York was more concerned with its geographical expansion and economic development than with cultivating the arts.

The metastasizing growth of the American city both frightened and fascinated Europe. After the city commissioners designed the gridiron plan for Manhattan in 1811, the task of scribbling in the blanks was essentially left in private hands. There was no centralized city planning comparable to Haussmann's in Paris. The geographical expansion of the city was "limited only by gross physical obstacles and the need of rapid urban transportation," as Lewis Mumford noted in 1961.[16] When Whitman was born in a small Long Island village in 1819, Canal Street represented the northernmost limit of Manhattan; beyond that limit, there were farms, open pastures, and forests. When the third edition of *Leaves of Grass* appeared in 1860, the city limits had moved up to Forty-Second Street. By the turn of the century, a decade after Whitman's death, all of Manhattan Island had been built over.[17] The turnover was rapid and often unpredictable. "Let us level to the earth all the houses that were not built within the last ten years; let us raise the devil and break things!": such was the unspoken but all too real motto of New York, according to Whitman.[18]

The unsettled and volatile identity of New York in the nineteenth century was not simply the result of what Whitman termed "the pull-down-and-build-over spirit." It was also the consequence of the unprecedented influx of immigrants from the "Old World" of Europe.[19] The American metropolis expanded at a vertiginous speed. By midcentury, New York had been half the size of Paris; in 1860, the American city, with over a million inhabitants, had caught up with the French capital.[20] The population of New York soared from 220,000 in the 1820s to 2.5 million by the end of the century. Such a sudden expansion, at a pace that was almost unimaginable by European standards, created deep social and cultural divisions within the city. Throughout Whitman's life in New York, the rift only grew wider between the businessmen, bankers, landlords, and political bosses at the upper echelons of New York society, and the increasingly large underclass that crammed the tenements on the southern tip of Manhattan Island.[21] The greatest wealth was juxtaposed with the most extreme misery. Between those who tried to survive in a world of low wages, high rents, periodic unemployment, and daily violence, and the Astors, Vanderbilts, Roosevelts, Rhinelanders, or Schermerhorns who lived in the princely townhouses that were being built on upper Broadway and Fifth Avenue, the contrast was almost unimaginable.

In his perambulations from Broadway to the Bowery, Whitman was confronted, day after day, and year after year, with the startling spectacle of "people of all classes and stages of rank—from all countries on the globe—engaged in all the varieties of avocations—of every grade, every hue of ignorance and learning, morality and vice, wealth and want, fashion and coarseness, breeding and brutality."[22] New York was chaotic, insalubrious, dangerous, and plagued with a sickening level of corruption. Whitman's city had the highest death rate in the world. At the same time, the city offered a startling display of modernity and wealth. The best hotels on Broadway were equipped with steam heat, gaslight, and indoor plumbing, which made them far more modern than their counterparts in London or Paris. But when Charles Dickens visited New York in 1842, the half-amused, half-disgusted novelist noted that hogs were busy scavenging in the middle of the city's most prosperous thoroughfare, mingling with the fine horse-drawn carriages and elegantly dressed ladies.[23]

As a journalist in New York in the 1840s and 1850s, Whitman was all too aware of the contradictory aspects of his city. Wandering through Manhattan and Brooklyn was one of his favorite pastimes. When he was working for the *New York Aurora* in the spring of 1842, at the age of twenty-two, Whitman would spend at least two hours every day walking in Battery Park or up and down Broadway, sporting, as one contemporary noticed, a dandy's attire of frock coat, high hat, boutonniere, and "dark, beautifully polished" cane.[24] In "The Painter of Modern Life," his celebrated essay on Constantin Guys, "artist, man of the world, man of crowds," Baudelaire defines the dandy as the last vestige of glorious aristocratic times in a world that is being leveled by the rising tide of democracy. Baudelaire finds a surprising example of dandyism in the New World: "Dandyism is the last flicker of heroism in decadent ages; and the sort of dandy discovered by the traveler in North America in no way in-a crepuscular, frightening, and corrupt city. Danger lurks at every corner: murderers, prostitutes, and thieves prowl the streets and boulevards, looking for prey. But the victims are always complicit in the crime. In Baudelaire's view, corruption and a frenzied thirst for pleasure have crushed the last vestiges of innocence in the city. All that remains is a perverse desire to destroy oneself and others as quickly and as painfully as possible. Despite his dissatisfactions, which grew more and more numerous in his late years, Walt Whitman would have viewed Baudelaire's pessimistic view of city life as an overstatement. In all of his verse, Whitman placed his faith in New York above his doubts. "Yet incessantly asking, yet I adhere to my city / Day upon day and year upon year, O City walking your streets," he exclaimed in "Give Me the Splendid Silent Sun," a patriotic poem composed during the Civil War. In another poem from the time of the Civil War, he reiterated his unconditional love for New York: "I have rejected nothing you have offered me. . . . / Good or bad I never question you—I love all—I do not condemn anything."

Posterity has retained the image of Whitman as an optimistic and exuberant bard who mythologized his chaotic city in his poetry. Tall buildings are metamorphosed into organic "high growths of iron, slender, strong, light, splendidly uprising towards clear skies."[32] Even the factories staining the shores of Brooklyn look beautiful, with their "foundry chimneys burning high and glaringly into the night." The crowds of New York are not bisected by the rift between the very rich and the very poor; they flow harmoniously up and down Broadway and the Battery. Every aspect of New York life becomes a source of wonder. Whitman revisits his city throughout *Leaves of Grass,* constantly finding new objects of fascination, no matter how ordinary they may seem:

> This is the city and I am one of the citizens,
> Whatever interests the rest interests me, politics, wars, markets,
>   newspapers, schools,
> The mayor and councils, banks, tariffs, steamships, factories, stocks,
>   stores, real estate and personal estate.[33]

The already long list could potentially go on forever. Whether he is sauntering down Broadway to gawk at the cacophonous display of fashion, commerce, and amusement, walking around the harbor, sitting on top of an omnibus, or standing on the deck of a ferryboat, Whitman is absorbing all aspects of city life within his "omnivorous" self and listing them one after the other. In his notebooks, he jotted down his idea for a poem entitled "A City Walk," which would have consisted in "Just a list of all that is seen in a walk through the streets of Brooklyn and New York and crossing the Ferry."[34]

Critics have insisted that this process of democratic inclusion is what defined the experience of the New York crowd in *Leaves of Grass*. As Peter Conrad has argued, Whitman "generates the crowd" and "incorporates its masses into himself. The athletic, ecstatic body inside which he thrives is a body politic. His fellow citizens on Broadway or the Brooklyn Ferry are members, literally physical components, of Whitman."[35] Alan Trachtenberg has shown that the poet's urban persona in *Leaves of Grass* erases all boundaries between the self and the crowds. "The lesson of Broadway," he has written, "its instruction in the mutuality and interdependence of I and you constitutes Whitman's poesis. . . . Whitman's city is the imaginative space where such things happen—not a place he represents but a process he enacts."[36] M. Wynn Thomas has pointed out that "the city was for Whitman the place in which the natural equality of men in 'their abundance of diversity' most torrentially and therefore irresistibly displayed itself."[37]

In Whitman's New York, landmarks recede into the background and the lives of individuals merge into a vast panorama. Whitman himself does not stand out in this gigantic cityscape, but vanishes into it. A ubiquitous instrument of vision, he assumes the role of recording the sights and sounds of New York, just as a photographer would assemble snapshots of the city in an enormous album. In his catalogs of city life, Whitman engages in an obsessive and potentially endless listing of details. Instead of imagining a fantastic and outsized creation, he seems to be merely listing the vital statistics of the city, stripping New York down to its most basic components. In truth, a nearly invisible archivist was concealed beneath the multicolored uniform of the rowdy. A transparent Bartleby had been peering out from behind the mask of the egomaniac. We are not shocked by "a triumph of confusion and religion of chaos," to use the words of Louis Étienne. Instead, we are presented with a radically simplified form of perception, in which sheer enumeration takes the place of imaginative syntax.

Whitman used his boast of being "of Manhattan the son" as a self-aggrandizing gesture of defiance. But there are signs throughout *Leaves of Grass* that point in the opposite direction. Whitman allows New York to push him out of his own poems, even as he incorporates the crowds of the city within his omnivorous self. He lets himself be cannibalized by the city that he calls "his." Whitman's poetry of New York is a self-defeating attempt to appropriate a place that cannot be claimed by anyone,

View of crowd in New York City Street, circa 1870. Robert N. Dennis Collection of Stereoscopic Views, Miriam and Ira D. Wallach Division of Art, Prints and Photographs, The New York Public Library for the Performing Arts, The New York Public Library, Astor, Lenox and Tilden Foundations

least of all by an idle flaneur. Many critics and readers have assumed that Whitman tried to normalize New York by gathering all its chaotic elements under the catchall term "democracy," but his poetry also accomplishes the opposite: it preserves the irreducible foreignness of the metropolis instead of making it acceptable to everyone and accepting of everyone. Throughout *Leaves of Grass,* New York appears as an uncharted territory—an open road that cannot be mapped out. There are no paths to follow, no landmarks to guide the traveler in his journey, no Mount Pisgah from which the whole island could be surveyed at once. No face stands out in the crowd. Through this maze, Whitman tramps a perpetual journey: "Day upon day and year upon year, O City walking your streets . . ."[38]

In an article written for the *New York Aurora,* Whitman described Broadway as "one incessant clang of omnibuses, carriages, and other vehicles."[39] A poem entitled "Broadway, 1861," sums up the New York thoroughfare in one line: "The ceaseless din."[40] The clamor of the street is so intense that it overwhelms both body and mind. The famous opening line of Baudelaire's poem "To A Woman Passing By" also places the poet at the center of urban chaos. "The deafening street roared about me," Baudelaire begins (to quote from Keith Waldrop's innovative translation of *Les Fleurs du mal* into proselike versets).[41] But for Baudelaire, unlike Whitman, there is nothing intrinsically poetic about street noise. The clamor recedes into the background of the poem, never to be mentioned again, as a silent apparition etches itself on the poet's consciousness: "Tall, slender, in deep mourning, majestically sad, a woman passed by me, one hand ostensibly lifting in balance her scalloped hem."[42] Time freezes as the ephemeral image of a woman in mourning obliterates the "roaring" streets of the city; and then the woman simply vanishes, leaving behind her an image of love destined to remain unspoken and unfulfilled. In Whitman's city poems, the din of the streets never ceases; time is forever rushing headlong into the next moment. Street noise forms an essential part of an oceanic flow of sound that connects the city with its crowds. It reverberates in the thousands of fleeting faces and fast-moving objects circulating in the city.

In "Mannahatta," the streets are "numberless," the masts of the ships "hemm'd thick" all around the harbor are "countless," the "trottoirs thronged," and the population of New York rises to "a million people." The streets that should provide the wanderer with a sense of direction are, instead, juxtaposed with the "tides swift and ample" and "flowing sea-currents," as if they were just as fluid and directionless. In an autobiographical reminiscence, Whitman compared Fifth Avenue to "a Mississippi of horses and rich vehicles, not by dozens and scores, but by hundreds and thousands . . . a moving, sparkling, hurrying crush for more than two miles."[43] Whitman the flaneur is not simply walking up and down Broadway, or traveling on the ferry: he is drifting down the river and letting himself be carried by the motion of the tide.[44] The scale of the city is not human, but oceanic. The busy commercial avenue that divides the city into East and West becomes the huge river that bisects the whole American continent. Whitman's city is so vast, so changeable, and so overwhelming that its effect on the observer can only be compared to that of the primeval American wilderness: an impenetrable enigma for the European traveler, a maze of secrets and of strange signs.

Throughout *Leaves of Grass,* Whitman refers to Manhattan by its original Algonquin name, "Mannahatta": "I was asking for something specific and perfect for my city / When, lo! Upsprang the aboriginal name." Long Island, where he was born, is restored to "fish-shape Paumanok" in his poetry. Whitman's appropriation of the Algonquin names, by then mostly forgotten, has been read as a way to ennoble the modern city by reuniting it with its geography and with its legendary past. Peter Conrad, for one, has interpreted Whitman's great urban ode, "Mannahatta," as evidence of "Whitman's victorious arrogation of the names and the place."[45] The poet (wrongly) translated "Mannahatta" as "the place of sparkling waters" and "Paumanok" as "the island with its breast long drawn out." The Algonquin names capture the essence of a land that used to resonate with sounds incomprehensible to Western ears— sounds that would have been described as the kind of "barbaric yawp" Whitman emits at the end of "Song of Myself." Names such as "Mannahatta" and "Paumanok" speak to a time when Manhattan Island and Long Island were still uncharted territories that did not appear on any maps. The name "Mannahatta," by itself, is meaningless in English; it can only be sounded, syllable after syllable. Since the Algonquins were believed to be almost extinct in Whitman's time, and since all traces of their civilization seemed to have vanished, the name "Mannahatta" is the only memory of a past that had long since ceased to exist. Whitman's "Mannahatta" is timeless, but not in the sense of cities like Paris or Rome. The timelessness of ancient European cities is archaeological: multiple traces of the city's history superimpose the past on the present and the future. When Baudelaire laments the modernization of Paris in "The Swan," one of the most elegiac of the "Parisian Scenes," he claims that it is impossible not to live in the past and not to be burdened by it in a place where "cherished memories weigh like rocks."[46] Even the most contemporary vision of Paris is anchored in the past. The physical obliteration of the "old Paris" in Baudelaire's time transformed the cityscape so deeply that some streets and quarters literally became unrecognizable. Yet their memory did not vanish. Baudelaire noticed all the scars in the cityscape, no matter how carefully they had been smoothed over by urban planners. He exhumed the rougher layers of the past underneath, even when they had become invisible to other eyewitnesses. But Whitman's hidden "Mannahatta" exists in a time that predates the beginnings of history. The Algonquin past has been so thoroughly annihilated that it is not even buried underneath the surface of the modern metropolis: it is simply gone.

An abyss separates Manhattan from "Mannahatta." The "perfect" name of the city can only be spelled in a tongue that now sounds like a foreign language. The modern Manhattan in *Leaves of Grass* tries to emulate an aboriginal language that has since been lost. Even as it seems to come to life with the most effervescence, Whitman's city exists only in absentia. "Mannahatta" is not the ghost lost somewhere beneath the surface of modern Manhattan. Instead, Whitman's Manhattan lives in the shadow of "Mannahatta." It is not that the ghost of the past is haunting the present: the present is itself the ghost. Whenever he describes "his" city, Whitman uses a shadow-language that struggles to approximate the lost speech of the aboriginal island.

From the time of its inception, New York had always been a polyglot city. However, Whitman shows little interest in the variety of languages spoken there. His New York is not primarily a city where many tongues and dialects collide. In this howling wilderness, sounds collide, clash, and crash. Toward the middle of "Song of Myself," Whitman claims: "Now I will do nothing but listen . . . / I hear all sounds running together, combined, fused or following."[47] He re-creates New York as a jumble of mechanical noise and anonymous voices:

> The blab of the pave, tires of carts, sluff of boot-soles, talk of the
>   promenaders,
> The heavy omnibus, the driver with his interrogating thumb, the
>   clank of the shod horses on the granite floor,
> The snow-sleighs, clinking, shouted jokes, pelts of snow-balls,
> The hurrahs for popular favorites, the fury of rous'd mobs.[48]

In this hybrid language, echoes of Paris and its boulevards reverberate in Whitman's New York. "Pave" should have been spelled *pavé* (for cobblestones), and "promenaders" is calqued on the French (the correct form is *promeneurs* or *flâneurs*). Whitman's recourse to French willfully connects the modern American city with its older, more prestigious counterpart, turning New York into a faint echo of Paris. At the same time, these foreign-sounding words, half-English and half-French, draw attention less for their meaning than for their strange, dissonant ring. Throughout this passage, human speech is enveloped in a chorus of pure sound: *blab, sluff, talk, clank, clinking, hurrahs*. In the draft of a poem about New York, Whitman spoke of "The heavy base, the great hum and harshness, composite and musical," which could be heard on the streets of the city.[49] The clang of New York streets makes the distinction between speech and sound irrelevant. Mechanical sounds both harmonize and clash with the echoes of voices that articulate no words and speak to no one in particular.

Reminiscing about his youth to his friend Horace Traubel, Whitman said that he particularly enjoyed declaiming poetry on top of omnibuses, in the middle of the noisy and crowded streets of Manhattan: "How often I spouted this . . . on the Broadway coaches, in the awful din of the streets. In that seething mass—that noise, chaos, bedlam—what is one voice more or less: one single voice added, thrown in, joyously mingled in the amazing chorus?"[50] In a segment of *Specimen Days,* Whitman remembers the days when he roared "some stormy passage from Julius Caesar or Richard" in the "heavy, dense, uninterrupted street-bass," while riding next to an omnibus driver on Broadway.[51] As he discovered the poetry distilled from the clashing sounds of the city, Whitman allowed his own voice to be overwhelmed by inanimate sounds, and by the "awful din of the streets." Absorbed in the flow of the crowds and in the sounds of the streets, the poet of New York could no longer keep up the fiction of a triumphant, boastful, all-conquering self. Stripped of his will, of his words, and of his body, he let himself become one of the "little plentiful manikins skipping around" on Broadway in "Song of Myself"—a ghost endlessly circulating through the streets and avenues—an echo chamber reverberating with the inhuman sounds of the city.[52]

Shadows and Daguerreotypes

In "Song of Myself," "you" and "I" delineate a public space in which Whitman's polyphonic self meets a crowd of other selves. All beings and all identities blend into a teeming receptacle, or empty shell, called "I" by the poet. Unlike what the title suggests, the "myself" of "Song of Myself" is not a self-contained "kosmos." Whitman is constantly assuming multiple and contradictory identities:

> I am of old and young, of the foolish as much as the wise,
> Regardless of others, ever regardful of others,
> Maternal as well as paternal, a child as well as a man,
> Stuff'd with the stuff that is coarse and stuff'd with the stuff that is
> fine,
> One of the Nation of many nations, the smallest the same and the
> largest the same.[53]

This monstrous ego, omnivorous and selfless, solipsistic and democratic, has puzzled generations of readers and critics.[54] Who says "I" in "Song of Myself"? What kind of substance—if any—does the poet have? Where does his self begin, and where does it end? Whitman urges the reader of "Song of Myself" to "unscrew the locks from their doors," thereby abjuring hypocrisy, disguises, and taboos. Placing his denuded body and his most private thoughts on display, he shows again and again how the intimate must become apparent, pointing to himself as an example to be followed. But it is precisely his exemplarity—the fact that he claims to stand for everyone, without any distinction or discrimination—that blurs this idiosyncratic self to the point of nonexistence.

In the celebrated short story by Edgar Allan Poe "The Man of the Crowd," first published in 1840, the convalescent narrator, sitting behind the window of a coffeehouse in London, watches the crowds hurrying along a boulevard. He entertains himself by deciphering their gait, dress, and expression, subsequently categorizing them as anything from noblemen, merchants, attorneys, and tradesmen, to clerks and professional gamblers. Then an old man appears, whose "absolute idiosyncrasy" arrests the narrator's attention. The man seems to be very poor, but he wears fine linen, and the narrator catches the glint of a dagger and a diamond through a rip in the man's ill-fitting overcoat. "How wild a history," the narrator exclaims to himself, "is written within that bosom!" The expression on the old man's face brings to mind startlingly contradictory "ideas of vast mental power, of caution, of penuriousness, of avarice, of coolness, of bloodthirstiness, of triumph, of merriment, of excessive terror, of intense, of supreme despair." The stranger, driven by a manic energy that belies his years, is followed around the streets and corners of the city for a whole day and a whole night by the increasingly obsessed narrator. The secret of the old man is hidden in plain sight. The narrator concludes that the man of the crowd simply "refuses to be alone." The "man of the crowd" derives his life force from the crowd as a vampire derives its life force from the blood of his victims. Perhaps it is best, the narrator reflects by way of conclusion, that the man of the crowd will not "let himself be read."[55]

Baudelaire, who translated "The Man of the Crowd" in 1853, brings up the narrator of Poe's story in his essay "The Painter of Modern Life" as a model for the pathologically secretive artist Constantin Guys. According to Baudelaire, both the real-life Guys and the fictional narrator of "The Man of the Crowd" are impelled by a compulsive curiosity. Having "come back from the shades of death," Poe's convalescent narrator, according to Baudelaire, "remembers and passionately wants to remember everything, as he had been on the point of forgetting everything." For "M. G.," as Baudelaire refers to Constantin Guys, indulging in the artist's morbid desire to leave no traces in writing, curiosity has also become "a compelling, irresistible passion."[56] We would expect Whitman, who compulsively follows the crowds on Broadway or on the Brooklyn Ferry, to be a more sympathetic version of the endlessly curious narrator imagined by Edgar Allan Poe and recognized by Baudelaire as the quintessential flaneur. But Whitman is closer to the wandering object of fas-

cination in "The Man of the Crowd." Walt Whitman the apostle of fraternity and universal love advertises his satanic nature in his most celebrated poem of New York, "Crossing Brooklyn Ferry": "I am he who knew
what it was to be evil . . . / Was wayward, vain, greedy, shallow, sly, cow-
ardly, malignant / The wolf, the snake, the hog not wanting in me."[57]
Rich and poor, innocent and criminal, triumphant and abject, a citizen
of all nations and of none, Whitman himself is "The Man of the Crowd."
Presenting an inscrutable surface to the reader, he refuses to let himself
be read. We can imagine that if Poe's narrator had ever caught up with
the man of the crowd, and looked closely at his face, he might have seen
the blue eyes of Walt Whitman, his white beard, and his unreadable
heart. As he was translating Poe's story, Baudelaire was looking at the
same man without being aware of it.[58] We can think, poetically, that behind Edgar Allan Poe stands the shadowy figure of Walt Whitman.

Although they both spent hours every day strolling through their
cities, and then writing journalistic accounts of their perambulations,
Edgar Allan Poe and Walt Whitman are rarely pictured together as fellow
flaneurs. In the early 1840s, when Whitman was working as a journalist
and editor, Poe composed a series of letters about New York for a now-
forgotten Pennsylvania newspaper, the *Columbia Spy*. He reported on a
broad range of topics, from the filth and noise of the streets to the spectacular growth of Brooklyn and the latest literary gossip.[59] Even if Poe
and Whitman both wrote articles about New York from the point of view
of fascinated but wary observers, we expect them to appear as polar op-
posites in their literary writings—one the epitome of darkness, the other
a luminous presence. Like Poe's fictional detective Auguste Dupin, the
narrator in "The Man of the Crowd" is looking for insoluble riddles in
the streets of the city. Poe's characters are drawn to puzzles for their own
sake, whereas Whitman the tireless flaneur seems to find bliss in the swift
resolution of dilemmas. Whitman apparently found the answers to the
questions he was obsessively asking himself as he walked up and down
Broadway or stood on the deck of ferryboats. This, at least, is what he
would have us believe.

"Crossing Brooklyn Ferry" appears to tell, far from the deviousness of
Poe's story, the least enigmatic and most straightforwardly optimistic of
stories. Set on the ferryboat carrying commuters back from Manhattan
to Brooklyn at sunset, "Crossing Brooklyn Ferry" offers a fluid, rhapsodic
meditation on time and identity. Watching the hundreds of men and
women on the boat with increasing curiosity, Whitman feels his own self
merging into the crowd, just as he pictures this particular moment in

time blending into many other such moments, both past and future. Anticipating that the crossing on the ferry will be repeated again and again in the future, even after his own death, he imagines that the passengers of the ship are bound to him by an invisible yet everlasting kinship. The river at sunset, the hills of Brooklyn, and the masts of "Mannahatta" standing in the background of the poem create a sense of spiritual elevation. To put it simply, a man is watching the crowd and finding spiritual bliss in this ordinary spectacle. This, it would seem, is the only secret in the poem, and this secret lies in plain view.

The poem is often read as a paean to the city and as an Emersonian celebration of the transcendent circle binding an individual to his fellow men and women. In 1899, William James pronounced it to be "a divinely beautiful poem."[60] Jerome Loving has written that "Crossing Brooklyn Ferry" represents "Whitman's greatest celebration of the transcendentalist unity of existence."[61] M. Wynn Thomas has made a case for the democratic egalitarianism at work in the poem, symbolized by the halo of light surrounding the poet and his fellow passengers on the ferry.[62] In the opening words of the poem, Whitman claims to derive "an impalpable sustenance" from "the hundreds and hundreds that cross, returning home," as well as from all the "sights and hearings, on the walk in the street and the passage over the river."[63] The tie that binds Whitman to the crowds of New York transcends the limitations of the present. The poem points to the future, "a hundred years hence, or ever so many years hence." Later, after many years have passed, another flaneur will also be watching these crowds on the deck of the ferryboat.

Yet the endless circulation of life in the poem ends in death. By projecting himself into the time of generations to come, Whitman anticipates both his own demise and the disappearance of all the men and women on the deck of the ferryboat. He speaks of himself in the past, as if he were already dead: "Just as any of you is one of a living crowd, I *was* one of a crowd."[64] In an earlier version of "Crossing Brooklyn Ferry," which survived in spirit if not in words through years of revisions, the poet already spoke of himself retrospectively: "But I *was* a Manhattanese, free, friendly and proud . . . / Saw many I loved in the street, or ferryboat, or public assembly, yet never told them a word."[65] As Dana Brand has pointed out, Whitman "represents himself as the only living person in the midst of a crowd of phantoms, or people who will be dead when the audience addressed in the poem actually reads it . . . yet simultaneously assumes the posture of the only dead person in the midst of a crowd of the living."[66]

At the heart of "Crossing Brooklyn Ferry," there is a secretive and faceless "Man of the Crowd," neither dead nor alive, who transforms all those around him into ghosts. Whitman never reveals himself to the other passengers, as if he were transparent to them. His invisibility becomes literal as he anticipates his own death. He draws his existence from his contact with the others, from their annihilation, and from his own:

> The impalpable sustenance of me from all things at all hours of the
>   day,
> The simple, compact, well-join'd scheme, myself disintegrated, every
>   one disintegrated yet part of the scheme.[67]

Whitman has no more substance than the image of thousands of ghosts crossing the ferry in a phantasmal future. His body firmly standing on the deck of the ferryboat, observing the urban panorama, becomes a ghostly reflection in the water: "Look'd at the fine centrifugal spokes of light round the shape of my head in the sunlit water."[68]

Like Charon's bark, ferrying the souls of the dead over the Styx, the ferry bridges the chasm between life and the Underworld. In "Crossing Brooklyn Ferry," what is most real is not the present. It is not Walt Whitman as he is crossing on the ferry—not even the crowds, both present and to come. What is most real, and most certain, is the most immaterial of all things: the subtle tie binding Whitman to all other men and women, the vision of still unborn men and women on the ferryboat. The present is merely a gap bridging the time of the past to a time when the world will be populated by those who are, as of now, not yet born. The men and women crossing from Manhattan to Brooklyn are crossing toward Death, "everyone disintegrated yet part of the scheme." The "real" world of the city is spiritual and invisible, like the air, the clouds, and the eternal motion of the tide—"The current rushing so swiftly and swimming with me far away." To be one of a crowd is to have already died.

In Baudelaire's "Parisian Scenes," elderly beggars, decrepit hags, and blind men teetering on the edge of the abyss haunt the streets and boulevards of the city. The obscene vision of a tiny coffin, as small as a child's, transporting the shrunken body of an old woman, strikes terror in the poet's heart. A remorseless murderer celebrates his newly found freedom from a quarrelsome wife before collapsing dead drunk into the gutter, while ragpickers pick their way through the waste of the labyrinthine city. "Crossing Brooklyn Ferry" displays no such monstrosities. There is nothing to remind us of the relentless horrors of physical decline, poverty, and crime; and yet Whitman's New York is as much of a necropolis as Baudelaire's Paris. Although Whitman wishes to make death "exhilarating," as he declares in one of the "Calamus" poems, his leaves of grass feed on dead bodies, not all of which are exalted or ethereal. As New York City's population grew exponentially, so did concerns about whether the "resulting waste, decay and decomposition could be absorbed by the natural environment."[69] A critic has recently argued that Whitman's obsession with death, which predates the carnage of the Civil War, reflected a growing unease with the intensification of urban density in New York at the time. In his journalistic writings, Whitman warned his fellow New Yorkers of the dire threat to public hygiene and health posed by urban burials and "the impure drainings of grave yards."[70] In a poem from 1856 published in the same edition as "Crossing Brooklyn Ferry," he expressed his fear that the festering dead bodies buried in the city might contaminate the living: "O how can it be that the ground itself does not sicken? . . . / Are they not continually putting distempered corpses within you?"[71] An ever-growing crowd of corpses threatening to push out the living crowds of the city: such an image lies at the core of "Crossing Brooklyn Ferry."

In an early draft of "Song of Myself," Whitman imagined himself playing the role of a shroud draped around a dead body:

> I am become a shroud;
> I wrap a body and lie in the coffin with it.
> It is dark there underground;
> It is not evil or pain there, it is the absence of all that is good.
> . . . .
> The retrospective ecstasy is upon me, now my spirits burn volcanic;
> The earth recedes ashamed before my prophetical crisis.[72]

In "Crossing Brooklyn Ferry," the ecstasy is palpable. There is an exultation in the sunset, the tides, the cityscape, and "the simple, compact, well-join'd scheme" of humanity. This, however, is the retrospective ecstasy of someone who has traveled to the afterlife and back. To loaf about in the city is to be immersed in the present, "the glories strung like beads on my smallest sights and hearings, on the walk in the street and the passage over the river."[73] On the ferry crossing from Manhattan to Brooklyn, or on Broadway, Whitman exults in the mere presence of objects and of bodies. He glories in the multiplicity of ships and carriages, of voices and sounds, of faces and figures. But this kaleidoscopic display of life is always a shadow. Vampirized by the omnivorous man of the crowd, objects and bodies disintegrate before they even have a chance to exist. They simply drift away and vanish. We have lost sight of their beginning and of their end.

Whitman's New York is a sphere whose circumference is nowhere, and whose center is everywhere. The island sits in the middle of an indescribable and unfathomable expanse. The poet's shifting and elusive "I" is no more a center than any of the multiple and fleeting voices surrounding it. His "call in the midst of the crowd" in "Song of Myself" is both his and not his; it could be issuing forth from any of the bodies in the crowd.[74] Alan Trachtenberg has observed that the call is "heard from without yet recognized as originating from within."[75] Any body—the body of any one—could be inside Whitman's voice, and vice versa. We no longer know who is speaking to us, or even if anyone is speaking at all. New York has become a parade of dreams. The world that had become so totally and so effusively present has lost its materiality. To "contain multitudes," as Whitman claims at the end of "Song of Myself," is to contain a multitude of empty and fleeting images.[76] Whitman's impulse to gather all the aspects of New York in *Leaves of Grass* leads to the inescapable unraveling of the city and of its poet. The crowded and ever-changing city is haunted by what Whitman called in one of the "Calamus" poems "The Terrible Doubt of Appearances." Whitman is a chronicler of the present, and of the presence of things; he always wants to touch, hold, and embrace. But he brings all that he touches into close contact with a death both his own, and anyone's. "Men and women crowding fast in the streets, if they are not flashes and specks what are they? / The streets themselves and the façades of houses, and goods in the windows."[77]

In his notebooks, Whitman jotted down the rough draft of a poem that would have been entitled either "Reflections" or "Shadows":

> As seen in the windows of the shops as I turn from the crowded
>   street and peer through the plate glass at the pictures or rich
>   goods.
> In Broadway, the reflections, moving, glistening, silent.
> . . . .
> The faces and figures, all so young, all so phantasmic,
> The omnibus passing and then another and another, the clear sky
>   up of . . .[78]

Whitman never completed the poem, but several versions of it appear in his notebooks. Another of these drafts reads:

Shadows of men and houses glistening.
A scene phantasmic spreads off before me, I see through the plate
    glass glistening.
Through the pictures of men and the landscapes over the pictures
    of the river-side and the ocean-side gliding over the tableaux and
    groups.[79]

It is not a coincidence that these fragments never added up to a finished poem, because the city is coming apart before Whitman's own eyes. Seen through the quintessentially modern material of plate glass, New York appears as nothing more than a flickering shadow.[80] The city vanishes behind a scrim of empty images and reflections. The glass windows may display a multiplicity of objects for sale, but what we see, most of all, is a constant stream of images moving on the surface. The city has turned into a procession of fleeting simulacra and ghostly images.

There are many reasons for this transformation, not the least of which is the sudden irruption in the mid-nineteenth-century city of a new kind of phantom. In July 1846, Whitman visited Plumbe's daguerreotype gallery on Broadway. The hundreds of "eyes gazing silently but fixedly upon" him created, he later wrote, "the impression of an immense Phantom concourse—speechless and motionless, but yet *realities*. You are indeed in a new world—a peopled world, though mute as the grave."[81] John Plumbe's gallery, located at 251 Broadway, in the heart of the commercial district, had become a fashionable spot for the urban flaneurs in mid-nineteenth-century New York. Daguerreotypes of eminent men and women—statesmen, artists, and performers—lined its waiting rooms, so that the living crowds that flocked to the gallery were met by a crowd of silent faces staring at them.[82] Plumbe's daguerreotypes captured human faces in hallucinatory detail, then lined up these faces on the wall, crowding them together as if the gallery were a crypt. Stunned by the precision of these portraits, Whitman was also acutely aware that photography had established a new and uncanny relation to death, even as it strove to immortalize the likeness of the living. His description emphasizes the interchangeability between the "real" person and the reflective surface of the daguerreotype, while also pointing to the abyss that separates real life from the image. A daguerreotype is both lifelike and the opposite of life. The long exposure times and enforced immobility required to fix the image on metal gave the models a lifeless and glass-eyed look. Because of the mirrorlike sheen of the copperplates, which were generally coated with silver, daguerreotypes, when held from certain angles, caused the viewer's own face to appear in the image, as if the spectator had been caught inside the world he was looking at. The people whose likeness was recorded for all posterity in these portraits were also transformed, in Whitman's eyes, into the image of phantoms crowding the concourses of the afterlife.

In December 1856, a decade after Whitman's visit to Plumbe's gallery in New York, the Goncourt brothers visited a photographer's gallery in Paris. They noted in their journal that "all these faces lined up and arranged in their boxes as in a coffin" reminded them of an "antechamber of the Morgue."[83] Because daguerreotypes were such a valuable and fragile commodity, destined to become, more often than not, a kind of miniature memorial, they were generally framed in flat coffinlike cases lined with velvet. In Paris, at the same time as the Goncourt brothers, Baudelaire also developed a profound aversion to photography, which he viewed as a grotesquely low form of technical achievement clamoring for the status of art. Photography enraged the fastidious Baudelaire because it ensured that no detail, however insignificant, would go unrecorded—and this not for the sake of art, but simply to satisfy a primitive delight in imitation. Anyone could be photographed and anyone could become a photographer. In Baudelaire's eyes, photography stood for the abominations of a democratic value system in which the crucial distinctions between high and low, art and entertainment, poetry and technology were about to vanish. Baudelaire denounced the "idolatrous crowds" rushing, "like one Narcissus," to see their own "trivial faces on metal plates." In his view, only poetry and painting could accurately represent a living being, precisely because their aim is to look beyond appearances, and into the labyrinthine world of the psyche. But photography could do no more than capture the empty shell of physical likeness. Baudelaire realized, as Whitman did, that photography and crowds, in some essential sense, shared the same nature.

Like Baudelaire in Paris, Whitman perceived the kinship between the crowd of silent pictures lined up on the walls of Plumbe's gallery and the similarly bustling hordes on the streets of New York.[84] Both saw that photography offered the promise of a potentially endless multiplication. But they also came to the realization that the images showed us our resemblance to ghosts. In the photographic display of silent faces in Plumbe's gallery, Whitman saw, as in a mirror, his own true face—the same face that he saw reflected in the kaleidoscopic visions shimmering across the plate glass of the shop windows.

TWO

This Insubstantial Pageant

Whitman is a very great poet, of the end of life.
—D. H. Lawrence, *Studies in Classic
American Literature* (1922)

Pageants and Panoramas

IN 1841, Phineas Taylor Barnum purchased the American Museum at the corner of Broadway and Ann Street in New York. The museum was soon drawing large crowds of visitors, eager to see its clamorously touted physical freaks, such as "General" Tom Thumb or the Siamese twins Eng and Chang. But the popularity of the museum also lay in the fact that it presented its attractions as theatrical shows, and not as a static collection of curiosities. In his memoirs, first published in 1855, P. T. Barnum referred to his attractions as "stage performances." They included, he claimed, "educated dogs, industrious fleas, automatons, jugglers, ventriloquists, living statuary, tableaux . . . pantomime, instrumental music, singing and dancing in great variety . . . dioramas, panoramas, dissolving views," as well as "American Indians, who enacted their warlike and religious ceremonies on the stage."[1] A passing remark made by Barnum, after he listed his varied attractions, also threw light on his phenomenal success: "The transient attractions of the Museum were constantly diversified," he explained.[2]

Whitman claimed to have interviewed P. T. Barnum for the *Brooklyn Daily Eagle* in May 1846, after the famous showman had returned from a triumphant European tour, during which his main attraction, "General" Tom Thumb, was presented to Queen Victoria. Asked to compare Europe with America, the entrepreneur allegedly answered: "There every-

34

thing is frozen—kings and *things*—formal, but absolutely *frozen:* here it is *life.* Here it is *freedom,* and here are *men.*" Whitman prophetically commented that "A whole book might be written on that little speech of Barnum's."[3] In *Leaves of Grass,* New York becomes Whitman's living American Museum—less a likeness of an art museum, if an art museum were defined as a collection of still, frozen images, than an image of Barnum's "constantly diversified" show. Whitman displays a series of living and moving images of the city, in which sights become shows, and seemingly immobile pictures come to life. The crowds do not provide a mere background and audience for the show. They find themselves, as newly invented performers, at the center of the stage. They are exhibited, displayed, and advertised as the main attraction of Whitman's poetic spectacle. With the same talent for self-advertising and self-aggrandizement as P. T. Barnum, the poet joins his living, breathing statuary on the stage, putting his own body and soul on display, rejecting social conventions, and sounding his "barbaric yawp over the roofs of the world" as if he were the carnival barker of the universe. Whitman's unconventional and spectacularly enigmatic persona, which was considered freakish by many of his contemporaries, is one of the many attractions on display in the great show of *Leaves of Grass.*[4]

In the century of P. T. Barnum and Walt Whitman, New York represented an apparently inexhaustible source of spectacles. A historian of popular American culture has noted that the city was "living theater . . . a place of processions, blazing lights, glare and glitter, fun and noise."[5] In *Low Life,* his history of old New York, Luc Sante points out that the nineteenth-century city was famous for its parades and rallies. "Torchlight processions took place every election night and on nearly every conceivable pretext—the laying of the Atlantic cable, the victory at Guantánamo Bay, the Feast of Our Lady of Mount Carmel, E. A. Beach's proposal for a municipal subway."[6] A poem from the 1860 cluster "Calamus," entitled "City of Orgies," celebrates New York for its "pageants," its "shifting tableaus," and "spectacles."[7] A pageant is a particularly spectacular form of show, emphasizing and magnifying its own artificial nature. A pageant stages itself, having no other subject than its own theatricality: unlike a play, it tells no story. Figuratively, the word means "an empty show without substance or reality."[8] The technically precise expression "shifting tableaus" shows how Whitman turns city sights into live performances. In dramatic terms, a tableau is a moment in a play, often before the curtain drops, when the actors freeze in a configuration that imitates a painting. Like a pageant, a tableau is mostly staged for effect. The "shifting tableaus" of New York can also be read as tableaux vivants, silent theatrical performances staging and imitating famous paintings. Tableaux vivants play a crucial role in Goethe's *Wahlverwandschaft,* in George Eliot's *Daniel Deronda,* in Edith Wharton's *The House of Mirth,* in Émile Zola's *La Curée,* and in the photographs of Lewis Carroll. Originally meant for the private entertainment of educated elites, tableaux vivants quickly found their way into popular culture, where they became also known as *poses plastiques.* They were a successful attraction in variety theaters in mid-nineteenth-century New York.[9] Tableaux vivants, living statuary, and pantomime were featured among the "transient attractions" of Barnum's American Museum.[10] Among a bewildering display of "panoramas of all the rivers in the known world . . . dioramas of the North Pole and of the gold-diggers of California . . . ventriloquists, somnambulists . . . and serpents of both the land and sea," a club in Victorian London presented a series of *poses plastiques.*[11]

The appeal of tableaux vivants for the spectator comes from the fact that they cross the boundaries between genres. Pageants and tableaux cannot be categorized either as theater or as painting, since they partake of both. As flesh-and-blood performers embody a still image, the frame of the painting is literally being removed. The staged spectacle of the tableau does not fall under the definition of "art" by the aesthetic standards of the nineteenth century. Tableaux vivants fit into a hybrid category, both broader and lower than art; and this is where the genre-defying *Leaves of Grass* also finds its proper place. Whitman always considered his poetry as a form of performance instead of literature. He repeatedly claimed, in print and in person, that *Leaves of Grass* was no book, but a living voice and a living body. Challenging those who would categorize his work as art, he strove to create the illusion that his poems sprang directly, like tableaux vivants, from his own body, and from the bodies of his fellow New Yorkers. As they cut across the boundaries between poetry, painting, and drama, his tableaux of New York transcend social and cultural hierarchies.

Throughout *Leaves of Grass,* the city's identity is generated by performance—not in the traditional sense of a well-ordered theatrical representation, but as an anarchic and unstoppable proliferation of images.[12] Whitman's metropolis seems to be spontaneously producing the spectacular shows displayed on its streets, squares, dead ends, and boulevards. By presenting this pageant as a self-generated phenomenon, Whitman obscures its origins and its mechanisms. The spectacle displayed on the streets and thoroughfares of New York cannot be traced to a single source; neither can it be described as the creation of a single stage manager or theatrical producer. Even if we assume that the pageant is the creation of the poet alone, this polyphonic and polymorphous subject resists all attempts to resolve its contradictions into a unity. Whitman's city is both Barnum the great showman, who creates, assembles, and promotes the circus, and the great Barnum circus itself. The boundaries between actor, stage manager, spectator, and spectacle dissolve. The configuration of New York lent itself well to such a blurring of distinctions. As Luc Sante points out, New York is a city "stingy with plazas and low on boulevards, built in piecemeal clumps rather than around a core [which] almost seems to have been designed to erase the distinction between spectator and spectacle, the only real separation being between the fixed and the mobile."[13]

In *Leaves of Grass,* the anonymous crowd on the stage is being watched and is watching itself at the same time. Since he is always in the crowd, the flaneur is, by definition, part of the show, even when he is watching it, or imagining that he is on the outside looking in. As he weaves his way in and out of the crowds, the poet of the city plays his part in the pageant of New York; but, at the same time, he observes the crowd from a distance, as if the spectacle were a panorama that revolved around him. In a letter written in October 1868 to his friend Peter Doyle, who may also have been his greatest love, Whitman described the "never ending amusement and study and recreation" of an omnibus ride on Broadway. "You see everything as you pass, a sort of living, endless panorama. . . . You will not wonder how much attraction all this is, on a fine day, to a great loafer like me, who enjoys so much seeing the busy world move by him."[14]

Reaching for an apt image to express his impression of the city, Whitman once again draws it from the domain of popular entertainment. A panorama was a large landscape painting or cityscape, which was unfolded before the spectator in segments, or unrolled around a cylindrical surface, with the spectator as a center. Like tableaux vivants, panoramas cut across the boundaries between painting and the theater. They replaced the frame of the painting with the illusion of a stage set, creating what some critics have called "a total illusion."[15] Panoramas had become all the rage in London and Paris during the last decade of the eighteenth century; they remained immensely popular until the last decades of the nineteenth century. Many panoramas were on display in nineteenth-century New York, and Whitman is likely to have seen panoramic views of his native city. Burckhardt's panorama "wrapped New York into a sectional circle and placed the viewer at its midpoint, while in E. Porter

Belden's you looked down on it, seeing it all at once like."[16] The panorama of E. Porter Belden, built in 1846, was a monumental carved wooden model of New York, which included perfect scale reproductions of every building in its skyline. A panorama aims at creating a sensation as sudden and as powerful as it is ephemeral—a shock that is experienced for its own sake, and not for the sake of art.

As he is riding on the omnibus or standing on the deck of the Brooklyn Ferry, Whitman is simultaneously observing the city as if it were a panorama revolving around him, and watching himself watching the cityscape. As in a hall of mirrors, or a circus fun-house, his gaze is both unique and infinitely multiplied. In "Crossing Brooklyn Ferry," he is observing the city and the crowds from a panoramic perspective, while simultaneously pointing to himself as "one of a crowd." He watches the passengers on the ferry from very close, almost from within, but also from a panoramic distance, as if "standing as on some mighty eagle's beak."[17] Seen "face to face," Manhattan and Brooklyn rise simultaneously on the horizon: "Stand up, tall masts of Mannahatta! Stand up, beautiful hills of Brooklyn!"[18] In Whitman's great 1860 ode to the city, "Mannahatta," the bird's-eye view includes the harbor, the streets, and the skies:

> Rich, hemm'd thick all around with sailships and steamships, an
>   island sixteen miles long, solid-founded,
> Numberless crowded streets, high growths of iron, slender, strong,
>   light, splendidly uprising toward clear skies,
> Tides swift and ample, well-loved by me, toward sundown,
> The flowing sea-currents, the little islands, larger adjoining islands,
>   the heights, the villas,
> The countless masts, the white shore-steamers, the lighters, the ferry-
>   boats, the black sea-steamers well-model'd,
> The down-town streets, the jobbers' houses of business, the houses
>   of business of the ship-merchants and money-brokers, the river-
>   streets.[19]

A "model of Whitman's all-embracing urban pantheism," the panorama allows him to "comprehend the city in a single omniscient survey," as Peter Conrad has observed.[20] The poet attempts to take in the whole city at once, looking from above at the "ferry-boats" on which he crosses the river and at the "numberless crowded streets" on which he takes his daily strolls. Whitman's catalog magnifies and embellishes New York, turning it into a gigantic maze of ships, streets, and vertiginously tall buildings; yet the city also appears oddly miniaturized, as in E. Porter Belden's panorama. The scale is off—both too large and too small. "Mannahatta" cannot fit into a normal scope of vision.

Gazing both from above and below, looking at the crowd and with the crowd, the urban observer keeps shifting his perspective on New York. By collapsing the distance between far and near, between object watched and watching subject, between actor and audience, the panorama of New York in *Leaves of Grass* erases the boundary between presence and representation. Whitman shifts the focus of perception from one subject perceived by a Cyclopean poetic eye to a multiplicity of objects perceived simultaneously by an eye that reflects and encompasses the Argus-like crowd. As Jonathan Crary has written of the new modes of vision in the nineteenth century, "There is never a pure access to a single object; vision is always multiple, adjacent to and overlapping with other objects, desires, and vectors."[21] The only faithful way to see, represent, or perceive a multiplicity, it would seem, is to become oneself multiple. Figured as a multiple eye, the crowd is mirrored in the equally avid and panoramic eye of the poet.

In Whitman's city show, an excessive and endlessly interchangeable self gives shape to, and is shaped by, a crowd that, in turn, calls for hyperbolic and superlative terms. The crowd cannot be delineated, defined, or broken down into its separate components. It overflows the boundaries of sense perception, going beyond the limits of our field of vision—beyond the limits of a poetic eye. Its chaotic vastness exceeds our ability to comprehend it, and annihilates our sense of proportion. In this sense, the crowd triggers the same extreme aesthetic reaction as the sublime, in the definition of Edmund Burke: "Infinity has a tendency to fill the mind with that sort of delightful horror . . . which is the truest test of the sublime. The eye not being able to perceive the bounds of many things, they seem to be infinite."[22] Like the vastness of the sea, a sublime spectacle par excellence, the crowd appears as an infinite expanse.

Although he never refers in his poems to the geometrical layout of New York, Whitman hardly ever fails to use oceanic imagery to describe the crowds of his native city. A poem composed in 1865 begins: "Out of the rolling ocean the crowd came a drop to me / Whispering *I love you*."[23] More than twenty years later, in a poem entitled "Broadway," Whitman compares the throng on the avenue to the tides around Manhattan Island:

What hurrying human tides, or day or night!
What passions, winnings, losses, ardors, swim thy waters!
What whirls of evil, bliss and sorrow, stem thee!
. . . .
Thou visor'd, vast, unspeakable show and lesson![24]

In a segment of *Specimen Days* entitled "Human and Heroic New York," he notes that "Broadway, the ferries, the west side of the city, the Bowery [are] bubbling and whirling and moving like [their] own environment of waters," concluding that the "myriad" people of the city are "on the scale of the oceans and tides."[25] The image may appear commonplace, if one thinks of such clichéd expressions as "a sea of people" or "a human tide." For Whitman, however, the mirroring effect between the crowds and the ocean is not a conceit. In Whitman's lifetime, the city's waterfront was much more visible than it is today. It was also far easier to reach the harbor from the city center and to walk along the island's edge. Manhattan's physical proximity to the ocean allowed the poet to "naturalize" the city, cleansing it of its filth, violence, and materialism.

But the haunting presence of the sea also speaks to the sublime vastness of the urban crowds. For Baudelaire, too, the crowds of the city and the boundless ocean are twin emblems of the "abyss of number" (*le gouffre du nombre*).[26] The crowds stand for the abstract, quasi-mathematical notion of a potentially endless multiplication that cannot be traced back to a single origin. The proliferation of men and women surging out of nowhere suggests a cosmic image of absurdity and infinity—the excess and nothingness of infinite space. Such is the terrifying vision that emerges from a desolate Parisian cityscape in Baudelaire's "The Seven Old Men," a poem from the "Parisian Scenes." Trudging along the dismal streets of the "Teeming city, city full of dreams" on a foggy day, "along pavements trembling under loading carts," Baudelaire catches sight of an old man dressed in filthy rags "the color of rainy skies." The old man walks, like a broken stick, with his legs and backbone at an angle. An identical old man appears behind the first one, then five more follow. Horror-struck, Baudelaire wonders whether he should be expecting an eighth old man, "ironic and mortal, disgusting phoenix, all-in-one son and father." Perhaps the eighth old man might have put an end to this ghostly procession, and finally brought to a close the process of self-generation that keeps emanating out a stream of crippled wretches. But no eighth old man appears: there is nothing but the unstoppable and pointless process of multiplication. As the poem reaches its convulsive end, Baudelaire, who now finds himself in a state of mental desperation, imagines that his soul is dancing "like a ship without a mast, on a monstrous, boundless sea!"[27]

Like the ocean, the crowds of the city fall under a category that Baudelaire called *l'innombrable:* namely, that which cannot be numbered, divided, or contained. Baudelaire's seven old men offer a small-scale image of Whitman's own struggle with number. By turning their attention to the city, Baudelaire and Whitman must re-create, in words, the shock of thousands of bodies, faces, and eyes—the terror of endless multiplication. The stage is so immense as to become almost immaterial, the panorama so vast that it is almost impossible to apprehend. Its sheer size makes it drift toward invisibility. At the end of "The Seven Old Men," Baudelaire locks himself in his room in a desperate effort to protect himself from the contagious madness he has just witnessed (or perhaps invented). Fearing for his reason, he refuses to look outdoors. He cannot trust his own ability to perceive the world, since the whole episode, ultimately, may have been nothing more than an opium-induced hallucination. Ultimately, the city signals the defeat of vision. The spectacle keeps exploding out of its frame. Fatherless men multiply on the streets, assaulting the helpless flaneur who stares at them so intently that he can no longer see anything at all. Whitman's body disappears within the thousands of other bodies in the crowd; his eye vanishes into thousands of other eyes. As he struggles to embrace the immense body of New York, his "insubstantial pageant," like Prospero's island, is poised to melt "into air, into thin air."[28]

Vanishing Points

In *Discipline and Punish,* Michel Foucault contrasts the "society of the spectacle" of the ancients, which allowed a large number of people to observe a small number of objects, with the modern "society of surveillance," in which very few individuals are presented with a vast panorama. For Foucault, the "Panopticon" of Jeremy Bentham—an architecture created so that a maximum number of people could be observed by a single set of eyes—came to embody the strategies of surveillance and social control inherent in the modern era.[29] Foucault's distinction between spectacle and surveillance rests on the hypothesis that there is a clear line separating the watching subject from the watched object. In Whitman's poetry of New York, this line reaches, so to speak, its vanishing point. More generally, Foucault's distinction between the ancient and the modern is challenged by the emergence of new models of vision in the nineteenth century, as Jonathan Crary has observed.[30] In an era of accelerating urban transformation, the body of the observer became the privileged site of experiments with perception, distance, and social control. Far from clashing, spectacle and surveillance collapsed into one another in the overcrowded metropolis.

In the summer of 1860, a Japanese embassy came to the United States to work on treaty arrangements between America and Japan. The event generated tremendous excitement, since this was the first occasion on which a Japanese delegation had come to the United States on an official mission.[31] In June, a military parade attended by hundreds of thousands of New Yorkers was held on Broadway in honor of the emissaries. To commemorate the event, Whitman composed an occasional poem that was published on June 27 in the *New York Times* under the title "The Errand-Bearers"—renamed "A Broadway Pageant" in the subsequent editions of *Leaves of Grass*. Ostensibly a paean to the Japanese dignitaries who have traveled halfway around the globe to parade on the streets of the American metropolis, the poem is also an ode to Whitman's beloved and familiar Manhattan:

> When Broadway is entirely given up to foot-passengers and foot-
>   standers, when the mass is densest,
> When the façades of the houses are alive with people, when eyes
>   gaze riveted tens of thousands at a time,
> When the guests from the islands advance, when the pageant moves
>   forward visible,
> When the summons is made, when the answer that waited thousands
>   of years answers,
> I too arising, answering, descend to the pavements, merge with the
>   crowd, and gaze with them.[32]

What fascinates Whitman in the poem is the juxtaposition of the "two-sworded princes, bare-headed, impassive" with the turbulent citizens of democratic Manhattan. In the eyes of the urban observer, the spectacle of the immense crowd filling the sidewalks of Broadway is as thrilling as the pageant of the splendidly dressed Japanese ambassadors. The "Broadway pageant" taking place on Broadway is also the pageant of Broadway. (A similar ambivalence presided over Baudelaire's choice of a title for his collection of prose poems. *Le Spleen de Paris* could be read either as the melancholy one feels in Paris, or as the melancholy felt by Paris itself.) In both cases, the city is an actor in its own narrative. Shift-

The Seventh Regiment arrives in front of the Metropolitan to escort the
Japanese Embassy to City Hall, June 18, 1861. Robert N. Dennis
Collection of Stereoscopic Views, Miriam and Ira D. Wallach Division of
Art, Prints and Photographs, The New York Public Library for the
Performing Arts, The New York Public Library, Astor, Lenox and Tilden
Foundations

ing the distinction between object and subject, Whitman speaks as observer of the city and as the city under scrutiny. He is both watching the
spectacle of which he is a part, and impersonating the city of which he
speaks. We no longer know whose voice we are hearing, just as we no
longer know what is being watched by whom. In "A Broadway Pageant,"
Whitman is hypnotized by the Japanese embassy, just like everyone else
in the crowd, but he is also observing the dense crowd watching the parade on Broadway. The Broadway pageant is a panoptic spectacle of mu-
tual surveillance: it is almost impossible to disentangle the crowd outside
the parade from the crowd inside it. The city itself, with its buildings and
boulevards, vanishes from view, as myriads of eyes define the scope of
Broadway: "The façades of the buildings are alive with people, eyes gaze
riveted tens of thousands at a time."

The eye of the crowd is self-referential; the city is looking at itself, just
as Whitman sees multiple images of himself in the crowd. The act of
watching is the spectacle, instead of being the medium through which
the spectacle takes shape. The word "spectacle" comes from the Latin
spectare, to look upon, to gaze at; a "spectacle," at its origin, simply means

the act of looking at something, instead of the thing being looked at. On the blank surface of Broadway, there is nothing to see, except for the spectacle of the myriad eyes hypnotized by the procession. The dense mass of the crowd both illuminates and obscures "A Broadway Pageant." Like an impressionist painting, the tableau blurs details and blends background into foreground so as to create the impression of self-generated, irrepressible movement. The relentless repetition of "when" in Whitman's poem implies that all actions are taking place simultaneously: the condensation of time keeps pace with the denseness of the crowd. But none of the words used to refer to what is actually taking place allow us to visualize either the spectacle or the people involved in it. Words such as "mass," "people," or "crowd" speak to the material presence of what they refer to; yet they have no connection with a specific mental representation. Even "crowd," which brings to mind the idea of multiplicity, signifies much, but shows little.

The Broadway pageant does not exist as a spectacle meant to be seen, but as a rhythm that articulates a nearly uninterrupted flow of perceptions. Sounds move in the space of the poem: they circulate, echo, and answer one another. Sounds answering one another, and answers being voiced in return, circulate between the crowd, the emissaries, and the poet. Whitman welcomes the foreign guests and the crowds of Manhattan into his poem, while answering the summons of "The Errand-Bearers." The organic rhythm of the city is based on hospitality, on reciprocity, on echoes and reverberations. A circle of sounds answers the New York crowd and the summons of the emissaries from the other end of the globe call. What had become invisible because it was too vast to apprehend in a single gaze is re-created in the drumbeat of the marching parade. The pageant of Broadway comes back to life in an echo chamber of jarring or matching sounds. The spectacle is not an image, but a reverberation, as if the crowd could only be perceived in its demultiplied echo. The panorama of the city is now a panorama of sound. What seemed almost impossible either to experience and to represent in words is suggested by making rhythm tangible.

Beyond their "visible" subjects, Whitman's poems are always evocative of a presence both before and beyond language. They always hint at something that precedes and overcomes the written sign—something that "print cannot touch"—a drift on the scale of the crowds, the oceans, and the tides.[33] In "A Broadway Pageant," the city, the crowds, and the poet exist in rhythm, and as rhythm, so that the visible world of the spectacle progressively vanishes. Instead of describing specific sights and sounds, Whitman presents us with a spectacle that could be characterized as an aural snapshot. In the poem, rhythm becomes something we can see; images become something we can hear; and motion, something we can almost touch.

Beneath the glittering surface of the pageant, an immaterial force is opening up the passages between the sensory perceptions. The power to see beyond the visible world is what one finds in dreams; and Whitman's New York is a dream city. The presence of the Japanese envoys induces a lengthy reverie about Asia, imagined as the "murky night-morning of wonder and fable inscrutable." As if Whitman were a Saint Anthony in Manhattan, hallucinatory visions rise up from the sights of Broadway: "Vast desolated cities, the gliding present, all of these and more are in the pageant-procession." If the Orient were defined as the country of fables and legends, it could then be said that Whitman orientalizes New York, telling himself fantastic stories about his native island, and transforming it into a place of "wonder and fable." Whitman metamorphoses the Manhattan of waking life into a phantasmagoric vision where past and future, phantoms and real bodies crowd into one another.[34] Whether the dream is something Whitman sees while he is asleep, or while he is awake, staring at the shifting pageants on Broadway, is an open question.

Whitman places New York at the center of a web of correspondences between the mundane reality of everyday life and the world of dreams. A fantastic vision brings together the archipelago that lies east of the Asian mainland and the island at the edge of the New World. The Orient is not imagined as the ancient and peaceful opposite of the frenzied crowds of the modern city, but as its mirror image. The fleeting pageant on the streets of New York contains an eternity: Whitman's dream city crystallizes old and new, past and future into a single moment. In the poem "Paris Dream," dedicated to Constantin Guys, Baudelaire imagines a dreamlike correspondence between the contemporary city and an imaginary Oriental palace. As if he had momentarily forgotten about the fashionable Paris encapsulated in Guys's urban sketches, he reinvents the city in the likeness of an immemorial Eastern dreamland. In the dream, the Paris Baudelaire knows has been transformed into a fantastic "Babel of staircases, or arcades. . . . teeming with basins, with cascades tumbling into rough or burnished gold." Traversed by "many celestial Ganges" pouring "treasure from their urns down diamond gulfs," this city seems "shining, clear, iridescent."[35] But the dream is short-lived: opening his eyes, Baudelaire finds himself once again in his wretched room, anticipating another wretched day.

Dreams keep on bursting into the world of Baudelaire's "Parisian Scenes," whether in the foggy light of day or the gaslit penumbra of night. The long, meditative poem "The Swan," which contains the only precise reference to Parisian topography in all of Baudelaire's poetry, is also one of the most dreamlike of the "Tableaux parisiens." Looking at a panicked swan that has escaped from its cage in the dilapidated area of the Carrousel near the Louvre, Baudelaire compares the swan to an African woman wandering in the muddy boulevards of modern Paris, and to the Greek heroine Andromache, sentenced to live in exile as a captive after the death of her husband Hector. We know that Andromache is dead, but it is impossible to tell whether the swan and the African woman are real or imagined. They can only be brought together in the poem because they are all dreamlike ghosts, living in exile, united only in their being out of place.

On the surface, Whitman's city seems to be offering the opposite of these desolate figures. His dream of New York is grounded in the fantasy of universal love and everlasting brotherhood. At the heart of his vision lies the assumption of an immediate and unending camaraderie—the presence of East and West, of past and future, at the same time, and in the same space. There is, to use a more Whitmanian term, an "adhesiveness" of all the men and women of the crowd that includes phantoms from the past and future. "Give me the Splendid Silent Sun," a poem from "Drum-Taps" that contrasts the stillness of the countryside with the excitement of wartime New York, vividly describes a military parade in Manhattan during the Civil War. Joining the "endless and noisy chorus," Whitman sees an endless stream of friends and lovers splintering out of the crowd toward him:

> Give me faces and streets—give me these phantoms incessant and
>   endless along the trottoirs!
> Give me interminable eyes—give me women—give me comrades
>   and lovers by the thousand!
> Let me see new ones everyday—let me hold new ones by the hand
>   every day!
> Give me such shows—give me the streets of Manhattan!
> Give me Broadway with the soldiers marching—give me the sounds
>   of the trumpets and drums![36]

Whitman projects the New Yorkers throwing themselves at him into the teeming panorama of his dreams. The identification of the observer with the city draws a solipsistic circle around the crowd. Whitman's yearning for "comrades and lovers by the thousand" is predicated on the unreality of such a wish. The pageant of New York revolves around an unfulfilled, unending, and unreal desire.

In another, much shorter poem from "Calamus," entitled "To a Stranger," Whitman's desire is no longer focused on the whole crowd, but on an anonymous passer-by: "Passing stranger! You must be he I was seeking. . . . / All is recall'd as we flit by each other, fluid, affectionate, chaste, matured."[37] Yet, here too, passing glances lead to no concrete contact, to no actual holding of hands, and to no final act of consummation. The two "chaste" strangers "flit by each other," but do not speak: "I am not to speak to you, I am to think of you when I sit alone or wake at night." Even in its title, Whitman's short poem is reminiscent of Baudelaire's celebrated sonnet "To a Woman Passing By." Both strike the same discordant note of melancholy and exultation. To use Walter Benjamin's stunning formulation, the poem is about "love at last sight."[38] But Whitman's poem, unlike Baudelaire's, is ambiguously gendered: at no point is the love object identified as male or female—although the allusion is transparent for any modern reader. The passing stranger's gender must remain unspoken because he is another male; and this reticence adds even more melancholy to the poem. Baudelaire's "To a Woman Passing By" makes it clear that the woman in mourning and the man who sees her will never meet again, except perhaps in dreams. The identity of the widow is an enigma, but nothing else in the poem is inexplicable, or too shameful to confess. Whitman can only hint at what makes his furtive encounter on the streets of the city poignant. The love he speaks of cannot be fully named, even less openly consummated. His romance with the stranger is doomed because it is destined to remain chaste. Sexual desire is reconfigured as a political vision of universal brotherhood.

On the surface, the city allows Whitman to form the image of a vibrant community of men. Thousands of strangers are offering themselves to other strangers. New York seems to be founded on the desire of one man for all the passing strangers in the city, and on their reciprocal desire for him. Both the city and the city poet are forever suspended in a state of never-ending youth, energy, and virility. Such an ideal lies at the core of the "Calamus" cluster of *Leaves of Grass*.[39] But the seemingly endless flow of energy in Whitman's utopian New York is shadowed by the uncanny realization that memories of the past and harrowing premonitions of the future contaminate the present. Whitman is making love, in his frenetic imagination, to the phantoms that walk the streets of the city. When he writes "All is recall'd as we flit by each other," he is not experiencing the present as a moment in time distinct from past and future. The present has already been lived in the past; everything has already happened. Whitman's own body is subjected to the same phantasmagoric metamorphosis. In the city where "the ceaseless crowd moves on the livelong day," he sees himself "effusing and fluid, a phantom curiously floating, now here absorb'd and arrested."[40] The fluidity of modern life in New York, which allows him to break down the barriers between himself and other citizens, transforms the bustling city into a strangely Baudelairian necropolis, peopled by phantoms watching other phantoms drift by.

Whitman's New York poems create the illusion of an instantaneous and everlasting bond between the citizens, but the city's passing strangers are so interchangeable that the bond between them becomes largely insubstantial. In "Song of Myself," the employees and businessmen on Broadway form a surprisingly sad parade of "little plentiful manikins skipping around in collars and tail'd coats." Whitman includes himself in the grotesque pageant: "I acknowledge the duplicates of myself, the weakest and shallowest is deathless with me."[41] To have been deathless will have meant, in retrospect, not to have been mortal at all; and, in the city, in the absence of gods, only ghosts are deathless. The mechanical parade of manikins on Broadway parodies the utopian community envisioned in "Give Me the Splendid Silent Sun," where passing strangers exchange "frequent and swift flash of eyes offering love."

Whitman's own dream seems to have turned into a nightmarish vision. In *Democratic Vistas*, Whitman's 1870 essay on the future of America, the city, placed under a "moral microscope" instead of being envisioned as a panoramic whole, becomes the pretext for a sullen jeremiad. In "Give me the Splendid Sun," Whitman claimed to love above everything else "the intense life, full to repletion and varied," of "the theatre, bar-room, huge hotel . . . the saloon of the steamer . . . the crowded excursion, the torchlight procession."[42] A few years later, in *Democratic Vistas*, he brands these places of entertainment with the mark of infamy:

> A sort of vast and dry Sahara appears, these cities, crowded with petty grotesques, malformations, phantoms, playing meaningless antics. Confess that everywhere, in shop, street, church, theatre, bar-room,

official chair, are pervading flippancy and vulgarity, low cunning, infidelity . . . everywhere an abnormal libidinousness, unhealthy forms, male, female, painted, padded, dyed, chignon'd, muddy complexions, bad blood.[43]

The vast and healthy body of New York has become a diseased organism, eroded by moral corruption and uncontrolled sexual desire. The utopian community of friends and lovers has degenerated into a parade of androgynous creatures. Even Whitman's ambiguously gendered sexual persona is being mocked in this grotesque blurring of sexual differences. Instead of the unexpected gift of love offered by strangers passing by him on the street, the city encourages a generalized sexual promiscuity that is perilously close to a universal prostitution, of the kind Baudelaire attributed to his own Babylon, Paris—"the gigantic whore," as he wrote in the unfinished epilogue for *The Flowers of Evil.* As if he meant to distance himself from his largely self-created reputation as a hedonist with loose sexual mores, Whitman is setting himself apart from the world of sinners, equating nature with moral purity and the unnatural with moral deviance. Unlike Baudelaire, who flaunted a perverse taste for "painted, padded, dyed, chignon'd" women, Whitman seems to be suddenly echoing Rousseau in his violent diatribe against the monstrously hybrid products of city life.

In his newspaper articles, Whitman complained with increasing bitterness about the immorality, filth, and violence of New York City.[44] It is as if he were speaking in two different and echoing voices. On the one hand, he metamorphoses the immoral, ruthless, and dangerous Manhattan of daily life into the beautifully renamed "Mannahatta," a name "specific and perfect for my city."[45] But on the other hand, he strips the city of its allegorical qualities, exposing it as the capital of sin.[46] One spectacle always hides another. The pageant is dazzling, but unreal: its tableaux shift almost seamlessly from the emphatically sublime to the inexplicably sordid.

On the surface, the pageants of New York in *Leaves of Grass* create the illusion of life, movement, and presence. But, at the same time, they work as smokescreens. The real meaning of the spectacle lies elsewhere. Beyond the visible configuration of the public parade, a larger and more abstract configuration is falling into place, as the shifting tableaux of New York solidify into a system of analogies and equivalences. In "Give Me the Splendid Silent Sun," the procession of Union soldiers celebrates the anticipated reunification of the American nation, as the Civil War was drawing to a close.[47] Whitman witnessed firsthand the horrific effects of the war as he nursed and comforted wounded soldiers in Washington hospitals during the war.[48] He was haunted by the idea of a rift within the United States, which would cause the country to split apart again. At the beginning of "Give Me the Splendid Silent Sun," he declares that he is "tired with ceaseless excitement, and rack'd by the war-strife." From his point of view, any threats to the young and still fragile American democracy would not come from the outside, but from the inside. In *Democratic Vistas,* he remarked on "the lack of a common skeleton, knitting all close," and expressed his "fear of conflicting and irreconcilable interiors."[49] As if in answer to these fears, the street pageant stages a spectacle of unity, which celebrates, in a literal sense, the approaching victory of the Union, and, in an abstract sense, the victory of union over strife.

Whitman, the crowd, and the marching soldiers are all allegorically united into a single "chorus." The streets of Manhattan, "with their powerful throbs," become a body through which a "throbbing" blood circulates, connecting and nourishing the organs. An image, in miniature, of the American nation about to be reunified, the city forms an organic whole—one body made of multiple, aggregated bodies, *E Pluribus Unum.* The New York pageant given for the Japanese embassy in "A Broadway Pageant" is also imagined as an allegory of reconciliation. Whitman describes the arrival of the Asian envoys as the sign that the ancient Orient is at last meeting its opposite, the young America:

> Superb-faced Manhattan!
> Comrade Americanos! To us, then at last the Orient comes.
> To us, my city,
> Where our tall-topt marble and iron beauties range on opposite
>   sides, to walk in the space between,
> To-day our Antipode comes.

The poem ends with an allegorical conclusion: "The sign is reversing, the orb is enclosed / The ring is circled, the journey is done."[50] Whitman fantasizes that the parade is the mystical accomplishment of a historical cycle, which manifests itself in a circular journey around the globe.[51] Such a vision aims to create a transcontinental and transhistorical illusion of unity. In "Give Me the Splendid Silent Sun" and "A Broadway Pageant," the tableaux of New York dramatize a historical and political situation. One nation and two continents are being reconciled, behind the scenes, and out of sight.

The poems may not be as abstract as they appear, then, since they allude to a specific political context. But Whitman's allegory of New York carries us beyond the political, into an eternal cycle that is inscribed in every aspect of the present. The parade on the streets of New York reads as a sign that eternity lies beyond history. The allegory points to death: invisible but omnipresent, death always lurks, as a shadow, in the background of the urban pageant. In "Give Me the Splendid Silent Sun," the sound and images of war merge into the images and sounds of the crowds on Broadway. The ghostlike soldiers who have just returned from combat, "young yet very old, worn, marching, noticing nothing," are mirrored in the "phantoms incessant and endless along the trottoirs." As the glorious procession of "A Broadway Pageant" unfolds, "vast desolated cities" appear in the background. In Whitman's frenetic New York, death and the crowd are not enemies, but allies. Seen from a panoramic distance, the members of a crowd are all alike, their myriad bodies pressed into one, their multiple eyes staring in a single direction. In the allegory, the dead also form a compact and homogeneous mass. No one is immortal; in death, the poem seems to say, we are all the same. Once our flesh gone is and dissolved into thin air, our immaterial soul (if we cleave to the promise of an afterlife) remains the only vestige of our past lives. This is how we should try to imagine Whitman's New York. Such a tableau of the city cannot be painted, since its degree of abstraction is so extreme that it would erase any living image. But the image always stands in the background of Whitman's poems of the city, as if there was, behind every tableau vivant, a *tableau mort*. In this configuration, ghosts are strolling together on the streets of the city, arm in arm. The crowds of the city belong with all the invisible things Whitman obsessively tried to translate into words—the surge and drift of waves, the odorless air in the atmosphere, the blades of grass on top of graves whispering to us the words of the dead.

Instead of inspiring fear, death unites and pacifies the turbulent crowds. But once these crowds are broken down into distinct individuals, and once these individuals, no longer assembled into a procession of shadows, suddenly come to life, then the city shows its most menacing face. Whenever the mask of allegory falls, Whitman's New York presents the unadorned spectacle of violence, poverty, and immorality. The serene vision of the crowds in "Give Me the Splendid Silent Sun" or "Crossing Brooklyn Ferry" stands in stark contrast to the collage of nightmarish visions of New York in the eighth section of "Song of Myself." Here, the mask has truly fallen. The individuals who appear in the poem form a gruesome parade of grotesques, more typical of Baudelaire than

of Whitman. We have been so accustomed to seeing Whitman as a re-
lentlessly optimistic poet that we are shocked by the raw pessimism of his
vision. By contrast, the violence of Baudelaire's prose poems appears distant and ironic. Baudelaire's stand-in fantasizes about beating up an old
beggar, or imagines himself murdering his mistress, but there are very
few "real" acts of violence in *Le Spleen de Paris*. The destitute people wandering through the prose poems are incapable of resorting to violence;
in his fantasy, Baudelaire has to teach the passive old beggar to stand up
for himself by forcing him to fight back. The violence of the prose poems
is so deliberately and pointedly grotesque that it often appears as a mere
outlet for Baudelaire's overflowing rage against the modern world—a
way of "getting back" at his contemporaries by imagining them in situa-
tions of utter helplessness.[52]

By contrast, in Whitman's catalog of city life, violence is painfully literal. It strikes without warning and most often without provocation. A
lunatic is "carried at last to the asylum a confirm'd case," just as one of
Whitman's own brothers was. A prostitute "draggles her shawl" while
"her bonnet bobs on her tipsy and pimpled neck," and "the crowd laugh
at her blackguard oaths." Far from the fashionable courtesans celebrated in Baudelaire's "The Painter of Modern Life"—fragrant women
with opulent hair and heavily made-up eyes, theatrically dressed in purple, orange, or scarlet—Whitman's diseased and drunken whore attracts
disgust and mockery. Another example of degradation is the opium
eater who "reclines with rigid head and just-open'd lips."[53] Unlike the
avant-garde aesthetes celebrated by Baudelaire in his *Artificial Edens* as
bold explorers cutting new paths toward unheard-of perceptions, Whitman's opium addict seems to be already in a state of rigor mortis. Drugs
do not turn sounds into colors, colors into music, musical notes into
numbers; nor do they allow the drug taker to perceive the minutest detail or most remote sound with the utmost clarity, as Baudelaire claimed
in *Artificial Edens*.[54] Instead, they extinguish any kind of sensibility to the
outside world. In "Song of Myself," Whitman speaks for those who can no
longer say anything. We hear the "groans of over-fed or half-starved who
fall sunstruck or in fits," we see the sick man being "borne to the hospi-
tal." The crowd even turns on itself, like a snake eating its own tail. After
"the meeting of enemies, the sudden oath, the blows and fall," the "hurrahs for popular favorites" quickly turn into the "fury of roused mobs,"
ready to launch into a riot.[55] The city seems close to disintegration. Bodies collapse, either from disease, violence, or poverty. Thunderstruck

bodies fall victim to haphazard events that are never explained, and never accounted for.

These glimpses of New York can be compared to a crime reportage or *faits divers*—lurid and unrelated stories involving a spectacular form of transgression. When Whitman was employed in New York as a journalist, newspapers presented a chaotic juxtaposition of material, ranging from the mundane to the sensational, from the elevated to the scandalous.[56] The French press was not exempt from this tendency: Baudelaire's poems, so canonized nowadays, appeared in the midst of trivial articles that are now totally forgotten, but certainly mattered far more to the readers (and journalists) at the time. More often than not, the poems were printed with typographical errors that caused the ever-touchy Baudelaire to vent his rage on his editors. He was particularly incensed by the fact that the French newspapers (much as they still do today) devoted an unusual amount of attention to events unfolding in the United States—as if this crassly materialistic society, which had hounded Edgar Allan Poe to death, could have any special interest in the eyes of the French public. "Belgium and the U.S. are the darlings of newspapers," he once observed with disgust, as if this were further proof of the spiritual inferiority of the American giant and of tiny, industrious Belgium—a country he saw as an American graft in Europe because of its devotion to commerce and political liberalism.[57] In spite of his abhorrence of the press, Baudelaire was forced to contend with the fact that newspapers provided a new outlet for literary creation, as well as a nonnegligible source of income for many writers.

In this sense, newspapers also became a template against which modern poetry, intent on delineating the features of the present, had to measure itself. Poetry could no longer ignore the disparate stories that clashed and collided every day in the press, recording all the dissonances of urban life. In "Song of Myself," the events happening on the streets of the city unfold in apparently random order. As Whitman himself "comes" and "departs," the scenes appear, then disappear just as rapidly, forming an improvised procession that stands in sharp contrast to the harmonious parades of "A Broadway Pageant" or "Give Me the Splendid Silent Sun." These vignettes of New York low life burst into the mind's eye, then abruptly vanish into silence. Voices are lost, die away, and then disappear. Whitman tries to rescue them from extinction; but all he can gather are echoes, as the real body of the city keeps on eluding him.

Like *Leaves of Grass*, the book that Whitman revised and rewrote until his death, New York could never arrive at any kind of completion. Either the crowds are about to vanish; or they are coming back from the dead so that they can speak to us in a "buried" voice. Nothing lasts. All we have, instead, is a vertiginous and kaleidoscopic acceleration of time. In "A Broadway Pageant," the procession is called "a kaleidoscope divine," a communal divinity that "moves changing before us."[58] Baudelaire, who famously characterized Constantin Guys as "a kaleidoscope endowed with consciousness," would certainly have savored Whitman's expression. Whereas Whitman's poems of New York are invariably defined by their physical closeness to their subject, the city and the crowds can only be perceived in the gap between an appearance and a disappearance— in the "sudden flash of eyes offering love," in the mirroring of a thousand eyes in Whitman's own clear blue eye, and in the echo of sounds buried in the stones of the city, and echoing again, endlessly suspended, in the voice of the flaneur. The interval is never breached, the contradictions never resolved. We will always see the city as an aftereffect. It will always be too late.

THREE

A Portrait of the Artist
as Parisian Prowler

EDMUND: Baudelaire.
TYRONE: Never heard of him.
EDMUND: He also wrote a poem about Jamie and the Great
   White Way—
TYRONE: That loafer! I hope to God he misses the last car
   and has to stay uptown!
EDMUND: [*goes on ignoring him*] Although he was French and
   never saw Broadway and died before Jamie was born. He
   knew him and Little Old New York just the same.
   —Eugene O'Neill, *Long Day's Journey Into Night* (1940)

Our Paris–New York

NO CITY IN THE NINETEENTH CENTURY was as radically transformed as Paris. Already unique in the variety of its architectural styles and the richness of its cultural past, Paris had been a capital of finance, administration, science, education, and the arts for centuries. But the urban planners of the mid-nineteenth century had little interest in archaeology: they wanted to turn the city away from the past and project it into the future. The renovation of the city started under Napoleon I and continued well into the 1880s; yet no plan for urban renovation was as systematic as Haussmann's. Between the mid-1850s and the late 1860s, Georges-Eugène Haussmann, prefect of the Seine district, working in close collaboration with the Emperor Napoleon III, carried out an unprecedented redesigning of the French capital. Many of the projects for the redesigning of Paris that had been left unfinished by his predecessors were finally brought to life by him. Under Haussmann's law, there would be no occluded pockets of the past trapped in the present day of a new Paris. All of Paris would be brought into the same moment, and it would no longer be possible to fall into a different time simply by moving into a different space.

Before Haussmann, the center of Paris was, for the most part, a maze of narrow, dark, and winding streets. This "Old Paris" would soon vanish both from view and from memory. Haussmann's general plan for Paris was to cut into its dense web of small streets so as to open large avenues that would facilitate the circulation between the recently opened train stations. The Boulevard de Strasbourg was cut through the city so as to improve the connection from the Gare du Nord to the Gare de l'Est. The Boulevard de Sébastopol, which ran from north to south, connected the Boulevard de Strasbourg on the Right Bank to the Boulevard Saint Michel on the Left Bank, and to the Gare de Sceaux. The new boulevard, which split Paris into two, was also meant to tear down the historical center of Parisian revolutions, from the rue Saint Denis and rue Saint Martin to the labyrinthine Halles district.[1] Haussmann declared with pride that "Paris was being eviscerated, the old Paris of the riots and the barricades, by the wide central thoroughfare that cut all the way into this maze."[2] Ancient streets disappeared, leaving no trace behind. Nothing remains today of the Place du Carrousel, so dear to Baudelaire, that stood between the Louvre and the Tuileries. This enclave of crumbling stones, makeshift shanties, damp passageways and standing water did not have its place in the modern Paris. The rue Transnonain also belonged to a past Haussmann wanted to obliterate: the site of an infamous massacre committed by the troops of Louis Philippe during a riot in 1834, it was razed in the redesigning of Paris.

In contrast to the old streets, the new boulevards were designed according to a geometrical pattern of long, straight, and crossing lines. Ancient houses, in Haussmann's eyes hovels, were razed to give way to the stately *immeubles haussmanniens*. The modern bourgeois buildings Haussmann designed were meant to confer a more orderly and harmonious structure on the city. Buildings were not to rise above a certain predetermined height, and their height was not to exceed the width of the streets, so that these same streets would never again fall into darkness even when the sun was still in the sky.[3] The transformations worked by Haussmann opened wide and brightly lit new vistas in the capital. Baron Haussmann claimed in his memoirs that he "never decided upon the design of any street, let alone of any main avenue, without considering first the point of view it would create."[4] With Haussmann, the city became visible as if for the first time, its outline legible for all to see. In the new cleared-out spaces, the perspective was no longer obstructed by the irregular layout of the streets, or by the uneven height of the buildings that lined them.

Haussmann's *grands boulevards,* as well as the public gardens he designed, such as the Bois de Vincennes or the Bois de Boulogne, created many ways of passing through the city, and made it easier for the crowds to circulate.[5] In 1801, Paris had a population of half a million; by mid-century, that number had more than doubled.[6] Before the *grands travaux* had carved a new life into Paris, the city had become more and more dangerous and congested. A cholera epidemic killed more than 18,000 Parisians in 1832. Forty years later, Maxime Du Camp, a celebrated figure in Parisian literary circles, wrote a multivolume work in defense of Haussmann's redesigning of Paris, entitled *Paris, Its Organs, Its Functions, Its Life.* Du Camp pointed out that Paris, after 1848, "was about to become uninhabitable. . . . Its population had been greatly enlarged and unsettled by the incessant activity of the railroad . . . and now this population was suffocating in the narrow, tangled, putrid alleyways in which it had been forcibly confined."[7]

The Old Paris formed a labyrinth of small streets, through which it was often difficult, if not dangerous, to circulate. In the labyrinths and dead ends of that enclosed space, passages were narrow, visibility was limited, and "blind spots" frequently left the traveler in a state of complete disorientation.

It was easy to wander, and to begin losing sight of what one was looking for. On the Île de la Cité, vividly depicted in Eugène Suë's serial novel *Les Mystères de Paris,* the cathedral of Notre Dame was surrounded by a dense accretion of mud-covered shanties and hovels, which gave shelter to a population of outcasts, prostitutes, and criminals. Haussmann destroyed this clandestine world, which blocked the view of the cathedral, and had its inhabitants expelled.[8] In its convoluted and hidden structure, the Old Paris was a mystery. After Haussmann's *grands travaux,* it became far easier to find one's way around the city, and increasingly more difficult to hide oneself within it. The cityscape was illuminated day and night. Gaslight had already been introduced in the early 1820s, before Haussmann, but it was widely disseminated by him.[9]

For someone who had taken pleasure in the secrets of the Old Paris, all this lighting elicited scorn. "Ask any good Frenchman who reads *his* newspaper every day in his café what he understands by progress, and his

Charles Marville, rue Scipion, view toward the Rue-du-Fer-à-Moulin in Paris. Ca. 1861. Adoc-photos / ArtResource, NY

answer will be steam, electricity, and gas-light," scoffed Baudelaire in his review of the World Fair of 1855.[10] Yet Baudelaire's *Petits poèmes en prose* incorporate many aspects of the modern Paris that struck him as grotesque, including the new technology of gaslight. One of the titles he had considered for his poems, *La Lueur et la Fumée* (*Glimmer and Smoke*), evokes a nighttime Parisian atmosphere: *la lueur* refers to the pale light shed by the streetlamps, as it pierces through the fog and smoke (*la fumée)* of the city.[11] The very first title Baudelaire envisaged for his new collection was *Poèmes nocturnes.*[12]

Even after the comforts of complete darkness gave way to a gaslit chiaroscuro, the night still offered a respite from the monotonous and well-ordered world of Haussmann's Paris. The modern city, which forced everyone to live in the present and to look ahead toward the future, made Baudelaire feel like "a decrepit old man" and "a mummy."[13] The new Paris shocked Baudelaire out of the past, which, in retrospect, became his true home. In the words of Walter Benjamin, "no one ever felt less at home in Paris than Baudelaire."[14] Baudelaire referred to Paris as "a nefarious capital," "a whorehouse," "a hell," and "a city . . . infatuated, to an atrocious degree, with pleasure."[15] In a letter to his mother dated 1862, he called the contemporary Parisians "a degenerate race," lamenting that the "charming" and "genial" litterateurs of the Romantic generation had been replaced by brutish and abject fools.[16] Yet Baudelaire hardly ever left the city where he had been born, as if Paris had cast a malefic spell from which he could not escape.

In the dedication of his prose poems to Arsène Houssaye, Baudelaire claims that the "obsessive ideal" of the *Petits poèmes en prose* "springs above all from frequent contact with enormous cities, from the crossing paths of their innumerable connections."[17] Baudelaire defines the modern city as a vertiginously open space (*villes énormes, innombrables rapports*) providing endless possibilities of "contact" and "crossing" (*rapport, croisement*). He does not create a distinctive image of Paris, even speaking of *les villes* in the plural, as if all cities were the same, and as if he was familiar with many, although Paris was the only city Baudelaire ever really knew.[18] The cityscape is simplified into the basic units of "the street" (*la rue*) and "the suburb" (*le faubourg*).[19] The latter term is ambiguous: *le faubourg* can signify a long street such as the Faubourg-du-temple on which the poet often strolled; or, more frequently, it can refer to the periphery of the city.[20] Baudelaire's faubourg, populated by beggars, ragpickers, drunks, and prostitutes, is almost always gray, bleak, and miserable.[21] The generic term *faubourg,* instead of reflecting a specific topography, evokes an atmosphere of gloom and sadness. There are no landmarks in the Paris of Baudelaire.[22]

Abstracted from its architectural structure and divested of its landmarks, Baudelaire's city is simplified—or convoluted—into a labyrinth of crossing paths: a mathematical game of chance rather than an identifiable place. As Walter Benjamin first pointed out, Paris and its crowds are barely described in Baudelaire's poetry, but they are every-where: "It is futile to search in *Les Fleurs du mal* or in *Spleen de Paris* for any counterpart to the portrayals of the city which Victor Hugo did with such mastery. Baudelaire describes neither the Parisians nor their city. Forgo-ing such descriptions enables him to invoke the one in the form of the other. His crowd is always the crowd of the big city, his Paris is invariably overpopulated."[23] Baudelaire's words do not describe Paris; they form, instead, an idea of the city. The prose poems from *Le Spleen de Paris* are consubstantial with it, as if they had emanated directly from its streets and faubourgs. In the dedication of the *Petits poèmes en prose,* the city is said to be *fréquentée,* a term that can be applied to either a person or a place. The city one "frequents," which is not the same as the city one lives in, does not essentially differ from the people one crosses on its streets. For Baudelaire, Paris is a place where crossing paths has become in-evitable. Everyone in the crowd is immediately visible to everyone else.

Secrets were inscribed in the labyrinthine structure of the old Paris, but the new Paris had become a public space, in which everyone was both watching and being watched. This is what the Goncourt brothers deplored in their journal entry dated November 18, 1860:

> My Paris, the Paris where I was born, the Paris of the mores of 1830 to 1848, is going away. . . . The interior is going to die. Life threatens to become public (*L'intérieur va mourir. La vie menace de devenir publique*). The club for those on high, the café for those below, this is what soci-ety and people will have come to. . . . Hence the impression of passing through these things, like a traveler. I am a stranger to what is coming, to what is, as I am a stranger to these new boulevards without turns, without mystery in their perspectives, implacable in their straight lines (*ces boulevards nouveaux sans tournants, sans aventures de perspec-tive, implacables de ligne droite*), which no longer smack of the world of Balzac, but remind one of some American Babylon of the future.[24]

For the Goncourt brothers, living in the modern city meant living in the public eye. The straight lines of the newly created boulevards eliminated on the one hand the possibility of random glimpses into other people's lives, and on the other the possibility of privacy. In their view, Hauss-mann's Paris represented both an advance and a regression. In a revised and abbreviated version of the journal, published three decades later, Edmond de Goncourt replaced the sentence "Life threatens to become public" with the more striking "Life is becoming public again" (*La vie re-tourne à devenir publique*). In Goncourt's view, the city was moving in two directions at once, both forward into the future and backward into the past. T. J. Clark points out that the idea of life "becoming public again" implies "a contradictory double time . . . as if the present public life was a regression from the fierce privacy which had hitherto characterized bourgeois existence, but also the form of the future."[25] By transforming itself into "some American Babylon of the future," of which New York was the paradigm, the new Paris was both reverting to a primitive state and becoming its own future.

Such a future was imagined as self-evidently barren of art, elegance, and fashionable conversation, since the worship of technological progress was incompatible with the love of beauty. The tyranny of public opinion in a democratic society, which horrified the aristocratically inclined Goncourt brothers as well as Baudelaire, enforced a systematic conformism that stifled beauty, originality, and talent. The architectural monotony enforced by Haussmann signaled the desire to engineer ideally submissive, spiritually dead citizens. For the Goncourt brothers as for Baudelaire, the modern Paris was not looking forward, but backward. They identified civilization with interiority, and interiority with secrets, implicitly acknowledging that there could be no literature without secrets. The notion of a modern utopia composed of an entirely public space, in which nothing would be hidden from view, made no sense to them.

When he exiled himself in Brussels toward the end of his life, Baudelaire simply could not understand why the Belgians placed so little value on privacy. He recoils in horror as he recounts that Belgian women urinate in the streets and defecate in front of their neighbors. According to him, the lack of a private sphere accounts for the spiritual desolation of Belgium—the primitiveness of its culture, as well as the uniform stupidity of its citizens. By contrast, the hidden and labyrinthine architecture of the old Paris embodies the positive values of complexity and involution. In the journal entry of the Goncourts, the Paris of the 1830s and 1840s is best represented by the complex, secretive, and mazelike structure of Balzac's literary Paris—a world shot through by secrets, deceptive appearances, and hidden tragedies. For the Goncourts, the simplification of the city under the aegis of Haussmann signified the disappearance of such intricate literary architectures. In the new Paris and other such "American Babylons of the future," people had become "travelers" and "strangers," as if their lives, no longer having any secrets, were comparable to the "implacable straight lines" of the new boulevards.

Baudelaire, who famously characterized the United States as "a gaslit wilderness" (*une barbarie éclairée au gaz*), strongly deplored the "Americanization" of Paris under Haussmann.[26] One of the traits he admired about Edgar Allan Poe was the American poet's contempt for soulless modern buildings. Baudelaire found comfort in the fact that Poe denounced the "*improvements* of human habitation," which were so praised by his American contemporaries, as "gaping scars and rectangular abominations."[27] In September 1859, Baudelaire wrote to Victor Hugo, who was living in exile in the Channel Islands and complaining of homesickness, that "one single day in our sad Paris, in our boring Paris, in our Paris–New York, would be enough to effect a radical cure in you."[28] The letter accompanied two quintessentially Parisian poems from *Les Fleurs du mal* that had been inscribed to Hugo: "The Seven Old Men" and "The Little Old Women" formed a diptych under the title "Parisian Ghosts." These poems express a nostalgic fondness for decay. The little old women, compared to "ruins," stand in for the rapidly disintegrating old Paris that surrounds them. In retrospect, the poems seem like desperate attempts to resist the monstrous "Americanization" of Paris, which was just then spreading to other parts of France. In October 1864, Baudelaire derided the harbor city of Le Havre, which was being modernized along the lines of Haussmann's Paris, as "dark and American" (to make matters worse, Le Havre was also the gateway to New York).[29]

Unlike the Goncourts, however, Baudelaire still found enigmas to be deciphered in the "Americanized" city. Baudelaire's prose poems have been collected under the dual title *Le Spleen de Paris* and *Petits poèmes en prose;* but some of the other titles Baudelaire considered, such as *The Parisian Prowler* (*Le rôdeur parisien*) or *The Solitary Wanderer* (*Le promeneur solitaire*), speak to his fascination with the secrets of the city. The old Paris may have been dying, but the new Paris had mysteries of its own. If the streets no longer offered the twists and turns so missed by the Goncourts, they provided ephemeral glimpses of "strangers" and "travelers." Crowds, unlike boulevards and buildings, had neither been neither wholly Haussmannized nor entirely "Americanized."

And yet Baudelaire's prose poems, which were composed between the mid-1850s and the mid-1860s, when Paris was being radically redesigned by Haussmann, have none of the richness or complexity as Balzac's Parisian stories. The *Petits poèmes en prose* simplify Paris into a surface without depth. Baudelaire's Paris, quite literally, is a "poor man's Paris." The three-dimensional, intensely private world of Balzac has been reduced to a cartoon scrawled on a wall. The difficulty of the prose poems lies not in their intricate structure, but in the fact that they give us fragments of public life viewed from the outside. Baudelaire drifts from one scene to another, and from one face in the crowd to another, without ever looking straight into anyone's heart. The modern observer of Parisian life still watches the crowds, but now he can only guess at their secrets. The secrets, however, are hidden in plain sight. The ultimate meaning of these scenes of Parisian life is a matter of conjecture.

In many poems of *Les Fleurs du mal,* Baudelaire unveils his own painful secrets, forcing himself and the reader to contemplate the labyrinths of his abjection. The verse collection invokes an intimate voice meant to be murmured aloud and memorized: *Sois sage, ô ma Douleur, et tiens-toi plus tranquille / Tu réclamais le Soir; il descend; le voici.*[30] The symmetrical beauty of the alexandrines maps these lamentations onto a musical structure. But in *Le Spleen de Paris,* Baudelaire is no longer holding up a mirror to himself. He is no longer wandering through his own heart, but through a desolate Parisian cityscape.[31] His gaze is turned outward, as if he had deliberately chosen to exile himself from the rich interior world of the poems in verse so as to launch himself into the impoverished exterior world of the prose poem. These poems follow no specific rules; they invent their own form as they go along. Some are very short, others almost the length of a short story. They escape both from the self-contained architecture of the alexandrine and from the claustrophobic confines of the self. The case can be made either that this daring formal experiment succeeded in shaking lyric poetry out of its lethargy, or that it announced an irreversible decline toward the prosaic and the banal. The same case—boldness or decline—could be made, on the other side of the Atlantic, for Walt Whitman's irregular verse and fondness for crude topics. Prose or proselike poetry creates its own logic; radical verse designs its own architecture.

In Baudelaire's case, liberation from formal constraints coincides with subjection to another governing principle, chance—the poor man's Fate in the degraded world of the modern city. No longer the privileged interpreter of secrets, Baudelaire simply chanced upon them.[32] The prose poems of Paris tell many stories of accidental encounters. The faces glimpsed on the streets prompt the observer to discern the secret architecture of the lives connected to each face. The secret architecture of physiognomy will also be an architecture of secrets. In "Miss Scalpel," the poet is drawn to an unknown woman he meets at "the furthest reaches of the suburbs, under the gas-light," because this apparition gives him the opportunity to throw some light, however ghastly, on a secret. "I am a passionate lover of mysteries because I continually hope to solve them. So I let myself be pulled along by this companion, or rather by this enigma beyond all my expectations" (*cette énigme inespérée*).[33] Baudelaire constructed *Le Spleen de Paris* as a labyrinth of tortuous and incomplete stories. He did not have the desire to build a structure as enormous and complex as Balzac's; nor did he have the ambition to cast a light on the myriad intricacies of Parisian society. With his enigmatic prose poems, Baudelaire was literally taking his chances. In his radical break from the traditional verse forms of *Les Fleurs du mal,* he was gambling that he could entrust his inspiration to the mystery of encounters on the streets of Paris.

An Architecture of Secrets

The crowds have their secrets in the new Paris of Haussmann, but the one who pieces their lives together has his own secrets too. In the very first entry of his private journals, Baudelaire writes:

> The pleasure of being in crowds is a mysterious expression of an ecstasy in the multiplication of number (*Le plaisir d'être dans les foules est une expression mystérieuse de la jouissance de la multiplication du nombre*).
>
> *All* is number. Number is in *all*. Number is in the individual. Intoxication is number (Tout *est nombre. Le nombre est dans* tout. *Le nombre est dans l'individu. L'ivresse est un nombre*).[34]

In the next entry, Baudelaire makes clear that the ecstasy of such a multiplication is a consequence of life in the new Paris:

> Religious intoxication of big cities.—Pantheism (*Ivresse religieuse des grandes villes.— Panthéisme*). I am everyone; everyone is me. (*Moi, c'est tous; tous, c'est moi*).
>   —Whirlwind (*Tourbillon*).[35]

Paris does not simply create a continuous series of collisions, shocks, and encounters between strangers: it also occasions a vertiginous exchange of identities (*Moi, c'est tous; tous, c'est moi. Tourbillon*). The self is found, as if by accident, in the pantheistic ecstasy of the crowds. Even the words for the experience of ecstasy and intoxication (*jouissance, ivresse*) suggest an escalating and vertiginous loss of self-awareness. There is joy in losing oneself in the crowds; there is an ecstasy in being finally outside of oneself. In "The Painter of Modern Life," Baudelaire argues that "for the consummate flaneur, who loves nothing better than to watch the world around him, there is a tremendous joy (*une immense jouissance*) in finding a home in number, in the fluctuations of the crowds, in the ephemeral and the infinite."[36] The ecstasy of the self in modern Paris consists in being displaced from the inside to the outside, from the one to number, and from the permanent to the ephemeral. By the middle of the nineteenth century, in Paris, the self is found, as if by accident, to be ecstatically the same as thousands of other selves.

The Goncourt brothers prophesied darkly of the "Americanized" Paris of Haussmann that the interior was going to die, and that both privacy and mystery would become anachronistic remnants of a past way of life. For Baudelaire, on the contrary, the ecstatic loss of interiority in modern Paris does not preclude the possibility of secrets. The pleasure of simply being part of a crowd is imagined as both "mysterious" and "religious." The ecstasy of modern cities, insofar as it transcends the boundaries of an individual self and replaces individualism with "pantheism," remains shrouded in mystery.

Strangely anonymous, existing almost at the edge of invisibility, the narrator in Baudelaire's miniature stories has no name of his own, like so many other characters. The old woman, the widow, the child, the old acrobat, or the poor (*la vieille, la veuve, l'enfant, le vieux saltimbanque, les pauvres*) have degraded into living generalities; they lack names and faces and anything else that would distinguish them from others of the same generic type. Naming would give a fixed identity to characters that make brief appearances in the poems, just as they make brief appearances in the life of the city. In this fragmented record of lives in nineteenth-century Paris, individual anonymity is an essential aspect of generic identity. The nature of the people in the crowd is defined by the qualities that connect them to other people of the same kind and class, and not by the qualities that would make them distinctively themselves. The "stranger" (*l'étranger*) who appears in the first of the prose poems encompasses all the other anonymous figures that briefly haunt the cityscape. Only two people are named: the clown Fancioulle in "A Hero's Death," and the "Beautiful Dorothea," who was based on a real Mauritian woman Baudelaire remembered from his brief stay on the African island, then called the Isle Bourbon.[37] Both of these characters are atypical of the people who drift through these poems. "A Hero's Death" is set in a remote and undefined past that is never quite identified as, but felt to be, the Renaissance; and "Beautiful Dorothea" unfolds against an exotic background that contrasts sharply with the clamorous contemporary setting of most of the other poems. Dorothea and Fancioulle are so remote

from Baudelaire's present—a moment in the middle of the transformations of nineteenth-century Paris—that their being named does not
make them any less strange, or any less distant.

Even those closest to the poet remain anonymous. The world of the
Petits poèmes en prose is intensely private, to the point of appearing her-
metic: Baudelaire refers to people and incidents familiar to him only.
The "friend" in the poem entitled "The Rope" is also the friend to whom
the poem is dedicated, the painter Édouard Manet; and the incident related in the poem did in fact happen to Manet. A young boy who worked
as Manet's assistant had taken his own life after being caught stealing by
the painter; and then the boy's mother had begged the distraught Manet
for a piece of the rope with which her son had hanged himself—not for
sentimental reasons, but in the hope she could sell it as a good-luck
charm.[38] The woman in "The Soup and the Clouds," who slaps the ab-
sent-minded poet for paying more attention to the passing clouds than
to the dinner placed in front of him, has been identified by some critics
as Baudelaire's last mistress, an actress with green eyes known now only
as "Berthe."[39] The unnamed musician in "The Thyrsus" is Franz Liszt, to
whom the poem is dedicated; Liszt was an acquaintance of Baudelaire's.
A private world is being made public here; but everyone's private identity
is subsumed into that of a public role as Baudelaire's mistress, friend, or
acquaintance. Everyone in the crowd of characters that populate these
poems is subjected to public scrutiny. At the same time, the poems retain
an intensely private aura, and names remain hidden in the crowd.

Baudelaire's own identity is equally elusive. He characterizes himself
generically as the "poet" or the "artist" (*le poète, l'artiste*), while also projecting himself into the figures of the other artists inside these poems,
such as Manet, the Belgian painter Joseph Stevens, and Franz Liszt. He
does not specifically praise Liszt for his music, but calls him instead a
"philosopher, poet, and artist."[40] Poets who simply belong to a crowd of
artists, have nothing more than the power to establish "innumerable
connections" with others. In "The Painter of Modern Life," Baudelaire
characterizes the artist and flaneur as "an *I* insatiably eager for the *not-I*"
(*un* moi *insatiable du* non-moi).[41] In the poem "The Crowds," he describes himself as a "solitary and pensive stroller" who "enters, when he
so desires, into the character of each individual," and "makes his own all
the professions, all the joys, and all the sufferings that chance presents to
him."[42] The voice of this solitary wanderer is heard every time Baudelaire
speaks in the first person. But this "I" is defined *a contrario* by an apparently endless porosity, which allows him to enter into "the character of

each individual" (*le personnage de chacun*). The expression comes from the theater, and the sentence can also be understood as playing "each character's part" or "everyone's role." Baudelaire will be playing the part of all these different characters, including even his own role as "the pensive and solitary stroller" (*un promeneur solitaire et pensif*).[43] The part will not be planned and written out, but improvised, according to chance and circumstance. In this spectacle, Baudelaire will put on a multiplicity of blank and anonymous masks, including his own. He will wear a mask painted with his own face; he will always be a stranger even to himself. The mask joins an absent self to other absent selves—a persona clamoring with other personae.

In the Paris of Baudelaire, the flaneur is described as "solitary" and "pensive" even when he is in the midst of the turbulent crowds. According to the terms of this description, "crowd" and "solitude" are synonymous, and not opposed. Baudelaire explicitly embraces the paradox: "Multitude and solitude: equivalent and interchangeable terms" (*Multitude et solitude: termes égaux et convertibles*), he concludes in "The Crowds."[44] In mid-nineteenth-century Paris, solitude becomes an experience brought forth by contact with the crowds. The privacy of a more old-fashioned solitude, the kind that the Goncourt brothers lament the passing of, appears almost unattainable. In the new Paris the crowds are always there. In the poem "Solitude," a journalist tries to convince the poet that solitude is morally wrong:

> I wish above everything else that this damned journalist would let me enjoy myself in my own way. "So you never feel the need, he asks me ... to share your ecstasies (*partager vos jouissances*)"? The jealous fellow thinks he is being cunning! He knows I have nothing but contempt for his pleasures, and he wants to worm his way into mine.[45]

Baudelaire can never be completely alone, as the outside world, in these Parisian prose poems, keeps bursting in. In a characteristically petulant mood, he wrote to his mother in 1866: "There is nothing I enjoy so much as being alone."[46] But the world would not leave him alone. Each of his prose poems offers a glimpse of the "innumerable contacts" that Paris imposes on the "pensive and solitary stroller." In one poem, a blissful moment of idle solitude is interrupted by a "horrible blow" on the door, which signals the nightmarish irruption of a bailiff and of a "notorious concubine." In other poems, a confrontation with the outside world takes the less nerve-racking shape of a passing encounter on a street; but solitude is still impossible.

The poems themselves cannot exist in a state of solitude. They are always going outdoors, into the city; or, conversely, the outdoors is always coming in. Some have specific addressees: poems are written to the poet's unfeeling mistress, or to his dog, which prefers the smell of excrement to the finest perfumes, or, even to all the wandering and homeless dogs (*chiens flâneurs*) that haunt the streets of Paris and Brussels.[47] In many poems, confrontations between two characters explode into gratuitous displays of bitterness, rage, or physical violence. In "The Bad Glazier," the poet wakes up one morning feeling dejected and bored. He notices an itinerant glazier on the street and yells for him to come up. He takes particular delight in the thought that the glazier will have to go up six narrow flights of stairs with his heavy load on his back. Once the glazier is upstairs, the poet demands the impossible—colored glass— feigning surprise and anger when the glazier evidently fails to comply. On a whim, he destroys the glass, and thus the livelihood, that the glazier is carrying on his back.[48] In another poem, a lover at a shooting range decapitates a doll with his gun. This was an easy shot, he explains to his mistress: all he had to do was to imagine her, his "darling angel," in the place of the doll.

These poems, created from the shocks inflicted by the city, exist in, and as, a series of confrontations with the outside world. The anonymity of the urban observer and of the Parisians he scrutinizes (none of whom return his gaze) is the postulate with which these poems both begin and end. Baudelaire, who revels in his invisibility, also struggles to break through the veil of anonymity. Each provocative gesture and stupid wager is meant to shake the audience out of its indifference. He both longs for and repudiates the ecstasy of complete solitude enjoyed by the self-sufficient Romantic poet. The modern solitude of contemporary Paris, for Baudelaire, is the painful ecstasy of the private colliding with the public. At work in these prose poems is a logic of instant reversibility, where joy becomes suffering, the private becomes public, and Baudelaire's own self shatters into the multiplicity of the crowd. Whether in ecstasy or in suffering, Paris always comes back to haunt Baudelaire.

The presence of Paris in these poems is so overwhelming that Baudelaire himself often recedes into the background, or even into nothingness. Just as he can never be quite alone, he can never be quite there. Effaced by the bodies of all the other characters encountered along the way, his own body seems transparent—a vanishing point lost somewhere in the endless avenues of the cityscape. The intoxication of the flaneur in the crowds does not herald the birth of a triumphant self, but signals the masochistic pleasure of a body offered to the pleasures and tortures of multiplication. Baudelaire does not incorporate all the other bodies in the crowd, but lets himself be vampirized by them. Baudelaire appears in some of his poems, but not in all of them. We come across him occasionally, as one would catch sight of a face in the crowd. In the course of *Le Spleen de Paris,* Baudelaire relates anecdotes of which he (or his stand-in) is the subject, but he also narrates incidents in which he plays the role of a mere spectator. Finally, some poems erase any visible trace of his presence.[49] In "The Rope," the painter Manet relates an anecdote in which the poet plays no part whatsoever; the poem is presented as the retelling of a story told by another, about an incident that happened to someone else. "The Old Woman's Despair," the second poem in the collection, and one of the shortest, tells the story of a kind-hearted old woman who looks so decrepit that she scares a young infant. As the baby she cradles in her arms howls with terror, she weeps. The poet appears nowhere in this cruel allegory of old age and enforced solitude. In the *Petits poèmes en prose,* Baudelaire has displaced himself as the subject of his own poetry.

Who he is no longer matters. All that matters is the fact that he happened to be here or there at such and such a time; that he witnessed a certain event; or that a certain story was told to him by someone he knows. Baudelaire's presence inside the poems is perceived as an accident, as is the sudden apparition of the poems inside him. Both forms of apparition are the result of chance rather than premeditation. Speaking of the prose poems he was trying to complete, Baudelaire wrote to Sainte-Beuve in 1866: "I hope that, one of these days, I will create a new Joseph Delorme, who will suspend his rhapsodic musings to each accident of his *flânerie* and draw disagreeable moral conclusions from all these encounters."[50] In *Le Spleen de Paris,* the self becomes anecdotal, even inessential, as Baudelaire's interiority is no longer the spur toward the landscape of aesthetic experience.

In mid-nineteenth-century Paris, experience is shared by all. People's stories, and even their innermost secrets, can be "read" and imagined; they can spread as rumor, or circulate in a newspaper article, penned by a "damned journalist." At the same time, as Walter Benjamin has shown, everyone is dispossessed of their own experience: "Experience has fallen in value. . . . Every glance at a newspaper demonstrates that it has reached a new low, that our picture, not only of the external world but of the moral world as well, overnight has undergone changes that were never thought possible."[51] Baudelaire steals people's secrets from them;

he feeds on their lives; he lives his own life through theirs, and they live whatever is left of their own lives, as if for posterity, through him. Baudelaire "enters into the character" of everyone, and plays everyone's role; and everyone "enters into the character" of Baudelaire in turn. Shared by all, experience is also shared by no one. Life becomes a cliché, a commonplace, a universal banality. The experience of life in mid-nineteenth-century Paris crystallizes in the gathering, telling, retelling, and collision of stories in the mind, ear, eye, and voice of the "pensive and solitary stroller," who "makes his own *all* the professions, *all* the joys, and *all* the sufferings that chance offers."

Legends, Clichés, and Dreams

Baudelaire's prose poems of Paris never appeared as a book in the poet's lifetime. In keeping with the practice of the mid-nineteenth century, when collections of poems were published in installments, like popular novels, they were parceled out to various journals and reviews. "I may have to give up trying to publish the sequel to the *Prose Poems,* although I had fifteen installments' worth," Baudelaire complained to his mother in 1862.[52] In 1869, two years after the death of Baudelaire, the prose poems appeared as a whole for the first time in the fourth volume of the *Oeuvres complètes* released by the Parisian publisher Michel Lévy. The editors were Baudelaire's friends Asselineau and Banville; the arrangement of the poems, still unchanged today, was based on a summary drawn up by Baudelaire in 1865.[53] The order of the current collection does not match the chronological order in which the poems first came into print: for instance, the celebrated poems "The Eyes of the Poor" and "The Counterfeit Coin," which were among the first to be published in Baudelaire's lifetime, are now numbered 26 and 28.[54] There is no certainty that the current order of the prose poems would have been Baudelaire's final word on the subject, especially since the poet was known, when it came to the presentation of his books, for his incessant demands and extreme fastidiousness.

As his letters to his publisher would have us believe, Baudelaire was planning to write one hundred prose poems; but only fifty were composed.[55] The prose poems that now appear before the reader's eyes are fragments of a work destined to remain apparently unfinished. In January 1863, he wrote to the journalist Mario Uchard that the prose poems were "almost finished." But in June he confessed to his mother that the collection was still very far from completion, although he claimed that all he needed was two straight weeks of work. In subsequent letters, he expressed yet more dissatisfaction with the poems, which he kept on rewriting and rearranging. Often, he despaired of ever completing the book.[56] Baudelaire blamed his inability to finish the prose poems on poor health, financial difficulties, and his drifting existence in Paris. After he settled down in Brussels in 1864, his move to the center of a monstrous nation was added to the list of his grievances. Baudelaire's self-imposed exile gave new meaning to the title of his collection. He noted in his journals that the only way to grasp the true nature of Brussels was to imagine what would have happened if Paris had been entirely taken over by the dullest elements of the bourgeoisie, and had remained unchanged since the last years of the reign of Louis Philippe. Forgetting his former complaints, he started feeling incurably nostalgic for the Paris he had left behind—falling prey to the "spleen of Paris." In the hellishly "Americanized" Belgium, Baudelaire felt that his private world, as well as civilization in general, were coming to an end. It was as if the abyss that terrified him throughout *Les Fleurs du mal* had suddenly become palpable. The unfinished prose poems were an image of the boundlessness of his despair.

In Paris, Baudelaire moved incessantly from one place to another, living at no fewer than forty-three addresses, including the kinds of furnished rooms usually occupied by migrant workers from the provinces and clandestine prostitutes. In a letter to his mother, dated April 5, 1855, he complains that he has had to move six times in a month: "As if all this was not ridiculous enough, *I HAVE TO* write verse in the midst of these intolerable shocks (*au milieu de ces insupportables secousses*) that wear me out."[57] In another letter to his mother, written in the winter of 1855, Baudelaire's exasperation edges into despair: "I am sick and tired of living in cheap inns and furnished rooms; it kills and poisons me. I don't know how I have survived this kind of life until now. I am tired of colds and migraines, of fevers . . . but above all of the snow, mud, and rain."[58] The city provided him with the fortuitous collisions from which he drew his inspiration, but it also inflicted upon him the shocks (*secousses*) that threatened to destroy him, and to make the writing of poetry impossible. Baudelaire conceived the writing of the prose poems as a constant struggle against adverse forces—most notably his "lethargy," as he termed it, and the "horrid city" that kept jolting him out of his concentration.[59] Their composition always interrupted, their completion forever postponed, the prose poems read discontinuously. They are, in themselves, an image of the chaos of Baudelaire's life.

Baudelaire always insisted that his verse collection *Les Fleurs du mal* was no "mere album," and that it had "a beginning and an end," as he wrote to Alfred de Vigny in 1861.[60] This statement has given rise to endless speculation about the "secret architecture" of the book. Baudelaire's own definition of his collection of prose poems was exactly the opposite. These poems, he claimed in the dedication to Arsène Houssaye, were made of interchangeable pieces, like the body of a serpent, or worm: "Remove one vertebra, and the two halves of this tortuous fantasy will have no difficulty in reuniting. Chop it into a number of fragments, and you will see that each can exist on its own."[61] With every new poem, the reader is taken by surprise and abruptly placed in an unfamiliar situation—like waking from one dream and finding oneself in an entirely new one. Each poem represents an ephemeral and distinct moment in time. Although Baudelaire claimed that the collection had been inspired by the "innumerable connections" formed in the modern city, he did not set all of these Parisian pieces in Paris. The poems clash with one another as if they had a life of their own—as if the author had simply chanced upon the disparate fragments of them in the course of his perambulations. Baudelaire provokes anyone who expects to find a discernible pattern into accepting that there is no point in looking for the "secret architecture" of the collection. We are invited to circulate among the prose poems as we would stroll among the streets of the city, taking in the sights and sounds as they come. The poems appear, then recede into the distance, as phantoms do in a dream, or in the innumerable passageways of the "enormous cities."

The events related in Baudelaire's prose poems never develop into a complete and finished story—a tale with beginning, middle, and end. Pieced together from details of people's physiognomy, gestures, and clothing, they are stories without a plot. As Baudelaire wrote in the dedication, what he offered was freedom. He was "not tying the reader's recalcitrant will to the unending thread of a superfluous plot (*fil interminable d'une intrigue superflue*)."[62] The stories are always plural, and always incomplete, as if they formed one and the same story, endlessly told and retold, with some variations, throughout the course of these poems. Told in pieces, they tell of experiences that are shared by a multiplicity of characters.

In one poem, Baudelaire imagines the stories of anonymous widows that he picks out of the crowd in a public garden. No one else is paying any attention to them. But he deciphers the sad tales inscribed on their faces:

A skilled observer (*un oeil expérimenté*) is never deceived in such matters. In those features, rigid or dejected, in those eyes, sunken and lackluster, or shining with the last glow of battle, in those wrinkles, countless and deep, in those steps, slow and ever so halting, he can immediately read the countless legends of love deceived, of devotion unacknowledged, of efforts unrewarded, of hunger and cold humbly and silently borne.[63]

Baudelaire breaks down the "crowd" of widows into clues—glimpses of faces and of gestures—that lead to a series of unfinished and interwoven stories. Like the crowd itself, the portrait of the widows is a collection of mismatched fragments. Their features are either "rigid or dejected" (the French *rigides ou abattus* suggests a more direct contradiction, since *abattu* refers to the relaxing of facial muscles that coincides with despondency, while *rigide* alludes to the tensing and hardening of the features). Their eyes are "sullen or glittering" (*ternes ou brillants*), their step both "slow" and "jerky" (*lentes et si saccadées*). In the end, these contradictions are resolved, because they do not characterize one person, but several. Baudelaire does not portray one widow, but puts together different pieces of the widows so as to sketch the composite portrait of a chimerical widow.

In the ancient world, the painter Zeuxis was famous for his portrait of Helen, inspired not by one perfectly beautiful woman, but by several models, each of whom was selected for the perfection of a single body part. Baudelaire's portrait of the widows offers a gruesome inversion of the chimerical image of beauty painted by Zeuxis, and proffered by Cicero as a model for a classical painter.[64] The "painter of modern life"—in this case, Baudelaire—pieces together the grotesque proportions and broken lives of unwanted and undesired women. A monstrous body replaces the classical model of a perfectly proportioned beauty. The "skilled eye" of the observer is attracted to the discarded human ephemera of modern life—people whose lives are so marginal that they remain cloaked in the anonymity of modern cities, and whose existence is so tenuous that their stories have to be shared in order to be told. Only then will they add up to a story capable of being heard. One of Baudelaire's most perceptive critics has observed that "The experience of the crowd is . . . humanity in its aggregate offering itself to observation. But this aggregate is not perceived as a totality; it is simply a composite multiplicity."[65] The "countless tales" (*innombrables légendes*) of all the widows add up to one story, which is always the same: a tale of poverty, betrayal, bitterness, and disillusionment. The widows' "unacknowledged devotion" (*dévouement inconnu*) means that they have obtained no recognition from those they loved, or even that their devotion is unacknowledged by those to whom they were devoted. Since they are widows, their devotion will have been vainly directed to the dead, who can neither know it nor respond to it. Their love will then have been "cheated" (*amour trompé*) by death itself, and not just by unfaithful husbands.

Baudelaire refers to the stories of the widows as legends, which sounds cruel and derisive if we have in mind the heroic connotations usually associated with the word, or even if we consider its Latin etymology—*legendus*, "that which must be read, that which should be read." In what way could the "legends" of the widows be imagined as exemplary, if not in an ironic sense? Although it seems as if they had already exhausted all possible forms of human suffering, Baudelaire inflicts one last wound on them by devising yet another way of blurring their lives together. The individual stories of the widows are replaced by stories that have already been written, and have circulated already for however long a time it takes to forget the true beginning of a story. In French, *légende* is also the word for a caption placed under a print or drawing, of the kind that were widely circulated in newspapers and displayed in printers' shop-windows in Baudelaire's time. Celebrated printmakers, like Gavarni and Daumier, occasionally wrote their own captions, but for the most part they were composed by the editors of the reviews in which the prints appeared, or even by anonymous assistants. In the poem "The Windows," Baudelaire watches a destitute old woman behind her window, and adds his own "legend" to the image he has cut out from the cityscape: "From her face, from her clothes, and from her gestures—from what is almost nothing I have rewritten her life story, or rather her legend" (*l'histoire de cette femme, ou plutôt sa légende*).[66] The legend still remains impersonal: Baudelaire does not write the life story of the old woman behind her window any more than he had written the stories of the aging widows in the public garden. Instead, he rewrites a legend. His physical disappearance from the scene of the poem mirrors his own self-effacement as the author of his own words.

In his journals, Baudelaire makes the following remark to himself: "To invent a cliché, that is genius. I must invent a cliché" (*Créer un poncif, c'est le génie. Je dois créer un poncif*).[67] *Un poncif*, the French word for cliché, literally denotes a stencil: a cut-out pattern whose printed image can be endlessly reproduced, circulated, and appropriated. The written words Baudelaire dreams of composing would become a "common property," a "commonplace." They would belong to everyone and to no one. With this new cliché, we would see the world in a certain way. The identity of the person who made us see the world in this light would be irrelevant. In another journal entry, Baudelaire claims that writing a poetic kind of prose implies the deliberate recourse to commonplaces: "Always be a poet, even in prose. A great style (there is nothing more beautiful than a cliché)" (*Sois toujours poète, même en prose. Grand style (rien de plus beau que le lieu commun*).[68] It seems strange that this credo could have been written by someone who was notorious for the extremity of his vision. In his writings on art, Baudelaire denounced the *poncif* as "a summary of vulgar and banal ideas." The very last words in *Les Fleurs du mal* are "One must dive head-first into the Unknown to seek out the *New*" (*Au fond de l'Inconnu pour trouver du* nouveau!).[69] But just as the new Paris, in the eyes of Baudelaire, had destroyed the notion of individual experience, it had also destroyed the idea of originality.[70]

The "legends" Baudelaire tells have a moral, as all legends do. Although they appear as mere anecdotes, their very insignificance points to something else. The fact that stories become legends, and that the attrition produced by the "innumerable connections" in nineteenth-century Paris leads to a devaluation of experience, carries moral implications. The fetishization of the cliché reflects Baudelaire's deeply ambivalent attitude toward his own time. Most of his prose poems, if not all of them, are allegories, however ambiguous or contradictory.[71] One poem allegorizes the predicament of the artist in modern Paris who has to sell himself to a philistine and vulgar public, a crowd drawn to the lowest possible prose, just as a dog is drawn to excrement. Another poem suggests, more mildly, that the poet of modern times is no longer surrounded by a sacred aura.[72] As he was working on these poems, in August 1862, Baudelaire wrote to his mother that he wanted to "flee Paris" and "the horror of the human face."[73] Baudelaire's legends are ironic because they do not elevate the poet above the common horde of other individuals. Instead, they place him inside the clichés of nineteenth-century Paris. The degradation Baudelaire attributes to the contemporary Parisians is also his own: it is the degradation of the unacknowledged and quasi-anonymous poet who has fallen into the mud of the boulevards, just like everyone else in Paris. Legends and allegories do not raise themselves—or their author—above the level of clichés.

Jean Starobinski points out that Baudelaire's allegories can be understood as pointing to the meaninglessness of the world that surrounds him:

One could contend that allegory manifests an excess, that it reveals the multiple "correspondences" that surround each "real" object. . . . But the opposite point is equally valid: when we can no longer perceive and acknowledge the real world as such, it becomes necessary to confer upon it another meaning, so as to prevent the disappearance of meaning itself.[74]

Baudelaire's clichés coincide both with an excess of stories and with the absence of real stories, just as his allegories do. The "real" world is no longer felt as a presence; it is rewritten as a legend. In "The Windows," Baudelaire retells the story of the old woman "from almost nothing." At the poem's conclusion, he writes: "Perhaps you will say to me: 'Are you sure that this legend is the right one?'" (*Peut-être me direz-vous: "Es-tu sûr que cette légende soit la vraie?"*). But the objective truth makes no difference to him; all he wants is for the legend to help him to survive, and give him the sense that he exists (*Qu'importe la réalité placée hors de moi, si elle m'a aidé à vivre, à sentir que je suis et ce que je suis?*).[75] The "real" woman is no longer the judge of her own experience. She has been entirely subsumed into her legend, and swallowed whole by the clichés sketched out in Baudelaire's retelling of her experience. The correspondence between reality and its description that can be defined as the "truth" (*le vrai*) has become irrelevant, along with the "real" world itself. Distancing himself both from truthfulness and from his own imagination, Baudelaire can only experience the world, and thus validate his existence, through another person's fictitious experience. But in the clichés that bring Baudelaire closer to his contemporaries lies the greatest possible gap between him and the world.

In the new, "Americanized" Paris, life is always mediated by clichés. The city creates "innumerable contacts," not between people, but between imaginary strangers who are no longer the subjects, or even the authors, of their own stories. The stories are secrets; but there is another layer of mystery hidden inside them. What are these legends of betrayed love and unacknowledged devotion? What is the story of the old woman seen through her window? We are never told. The commonplace legends the poet tells himself do not illustrate a visible image, or even tell a moment in a story; instead, they preserve the opacity of anonymous lives. The poems reveal dreams, daydreams, and reveries rather than "real" experience. Among the notes Baudelaire jotted down for the project whose final title would become *Le Spleen de Paris,* one finds, under the heading "Classification," the words: "Parisian Things. Dreams. Symbols and

Moral Lessons" (*Choses parisiennes. Rêves. Symboles et moralités*).[76] In the poem "The Double Bedroom," Baudelaire's room, colored blue and rose pink, perfumed with exquisite fragrances, offers an ideal vision of Beauty: it "looks like a daydream" (*une rêverie*). The room is then shown to be exactly the opposite: a typically Parisian apartment—dark, cold, cramped, and filled with the stench of tobacco and mold. Perceived first as in a dream, the "double bedroom" becomes inescapably real—that is to say, a "Parisian thing." Which bedroom is the "true" one? Paris, the "teeming city, city full of dreams," inspires prose poems that blur the lines between the world of dreams and the "real" world of nineteenth-century Paris.

Just as they do in the crowds, the self and the nonself come into contact in the world of dreams. Dreams are both our own and not our own; they are both familiar and unfamiliar, both clichés and uniquely, joyously, or painfully particular. In the third of the prose poems—an autobiographical meditation on the relation between the artist and nature—an artist watching a peaceful autumnal seascape falls into a deep reverie: "All these things think for me, and I for them (for in the grandeur of daydreaming the self is soon lost)" (*car dans la grandeur de la rêverie le* moi *se perd vite!*).[77] But his peace of mind soon gives way to anguish. By losing himself in the landscape he is watching, the artist becomes nothing; and this nothing no longer has the capacity to memorialize Beauty. "The contemplation of beauty is a duel in which the artist screams in terror before being defeated."[78] Like solitude—always an unattainable ideal for Baudelaire—daydreaming does not offer the promise of a withdrawal from the world. On the contrary, daydreaming marks the incorporation of the "I" into the "non-I." Artistic creation is not a production issuing forth from the inside—from the "inner world" of the artist—to the outside. It is experienced, instead, as the outside imposing itself on the inside, enveloping and dissolving it. In the process, the physical Baudelaire who walks on the streets of the city, losing himself in daydreams, and the artist Baudelaire who contemplates beauty only to be ultimately destroyed by it, lose their selves, and are left with almost nothing.

In a letter to Alfred de Vigny dated January 30, 1862, Baudelaire mentions in passing his "elucubrations in prose." Writing to Sainte-Beuve a few days later, he referred to his prose poems as "daydreaming in prose" (*Rêvasseries en prose*).[79] In the dedication to Arsène Houssaye, Baudelaire wrote that he had "dreamt of the miracle of a form of poetic prose . . . both supple and staccato enough to adapt itself to the lyrical movement of our souls, the undulating movement of our reveries, and the convulsive movement (*soubresaut*) of our consciences."[80] In this artistic credo, the idea of "dreaming" appears twice. The "miracle" of a poetic prose is defined as "a dream," that is to say, a goal that cannot be planned out or premeditated, but only chanced upon. Even before the poems themselves appear, Baudelaire confesses to the reader that they will always remain incomplete, since they will have been measured against the impossible ideal of the dream, which we enter into by chance, and fall from just as suddenly. The second occurrence of the word "dream" happens when Baudelaire invokes "the undulating movements of day-dreaming" (*les ondulations de la rêverie*) to characterize the subject of the poems. The "description of modern life," which forms, as he proclaims in the dedication, the main subject of the book, flows from physical movement, and from the sudden convulsion (*soubresaut*) of coming into consciousness.[81] In nineteenth-century Paris, the outside world takes hold of the body, jerks the dreamer into wakefulness, and then just as quickly launches him into yet another dream.

Most of the prose poems begin, as dreams do, in medias res. A person appears, or an event occurs, without any explanation. The very first poem in the collection, entitled "The Stranger," consists in a brief dialogue between two unidentified speakers. Although the man asking questions uses the *tu* form, which implies a degree of familiarity, he refers to the other man as "an enigma." Both remain wholly opaque to the reader. The stranger who answers the questions confesses that he has no family or friends, and despises money; the only thing in the world he loves is to watch the passing clouds. This poem, which presents itself as a dialogue, may in fact be an interior monologue—a conversation Baudelaire is having with himself; but it is impossible to tell. Baudelaire's twenty-ninth prose poem, "The Generous Gambler," recounts in a matter-of-fact tone an encounter on the streets of Paris with none other than the Devil: "Yesterday, amidst the crowds on the boulevard, I felt myself brushed against a mysterious Being whom I had always longed to know and whom I recognized immediately, although I had never seen him."[82] The Devil takes the poet to a magnificent apartment where they share an exquisite lunch, smoke cigars, and discuss world affairs like two gentlemen in a salon. In one of the last poems in the collection, "Miss Scalpel," a young woman suddenly accosts a man walking down the faubourg. This encounter is presented as a "natural" event, just as, in a dream, strange things "naturally" form narrative sequences over which we have little control, but which appear inescapable. "As I came to the furthest reaches of the suburbs, under the gas lights, I felt an arm slip gently under mine and heard a voice in my ear, 'You are a doctor, Monsieur?' "[83] As the flaneur follows this strange prostitute to her apartment, she keeps on obsessively talking about young interns and surgeons in their blood-spattered coats. Dreams are brought into waking life, both for better and for worse.

At the end of "Miss Scalpel," the enigma of the young woman's fascination with doctors remains unsolved. She clearly suffers from some form of madness, but no explanation is forthcoming, and the passing encounter will lead to no further contact. In "The Generous Gambler," the poet sells his soul to the Devil in exchange for the promise that his life will no longer be plagued by the agonies of boredom (*Ennui*). But, once he returns home, he doubts that the Devil will keep his word. Just as the reader cannot know if Baudelaire's claim of allegiance to Satan in *Les Fleurs du Mal* should be understood literally, we are left to wonder whether the poem itself may not also be a hoax. The poems pullulate with strange signs, which can be read ironically, allegorically, or simply literally. The *Petits poèmes en prose* are all placed under the sign of undecidability and ambivalence—there are no exceptions.[84] Miss Scalpel may represent the figure of the "innocent monster," and the Devil may well be a stereotypical Devil. But the stereotypical nature of these characters creates a new level of opacity and strangeness. Baudelaire stretches the limits both of verisimilitude and of morality. We are left to wonder whether we are supposed to take these poems seriously; we ask ourselves if Baudelaire's purpose is not simply to mock us. Baudelaire himself never elucidates the enigmas he has chanced upon in the midst of the crowds. The city brings the dream into waking life. The poems begin and end without reason, punctuating the dream of life in the cityscape of Paris with moments that seem like waking; but these moments signal to Baudelaire, to the crowds, and to the audience that their lives will never be their own.

FOUR

Dark Rooms

A Macabre Pantomime

BY THE 1830s, the Romantics, always eager to find new and unexpected modes of expression, had fallen under the spell of pantomimes.[1] In 1842, Théophile Gautier wrote a review of *The Used Clothes Peddler* (*Le Marchand d'habits*) for *La Revue de Paris*.[2] He was struck by the hybrid nature of this "strange drama in which laughter is tinged with terror."[3] In the pantomime, Pierrot falls in love with a beautiful Duchess, but since he is too poor to be introduced to her, he kills a used clothes peddler, steals his most resplendent finery, and meets the lady dressed in his ill-gotten gains. After some time has passed, and Pierrot and the duchess are about to be married, the ghost of the old peddler comes back onto the scene to drag Pierrot to his death. The role of Pierrot was performed by the celebrated mime Jean-Gaspard-Baptiste Deburau. The Romantic fascination with pantomimes such as *The Used Clothes Peddler* can be attributed in part to Deburau's charisma. Witnesses remember most of all both his feline agility and his uncanny stillness.[4] Pantomimes such as Deburau's told stories that left ample room for spectacular acrobatics. (A *funambule* is a rope dancer; when the Théâtre des Funambules opened in 1816, the actors had no choice but to make their entrance on a tightrope that led up to the stage.)[5] But Deburau, according to his contemporaries, carried the pantomime into a more ethereal realm. Théodore de Banville, who published a collection of poems called *Odes funambulesques* in 1857, said of Deburau that each of his pantomimes was like another rhapsody added to a single long poem.[6] The poem came to an end in June 1846, when Jean-Gaspard-Baptiste Deburau died. A few months later, Baudelaire and his friends Théophile Gautier, Théodore de

Banville, and Gérard de Nerval attended the opening night of a bleak pantomime entitled *Pierrot Servant of Death* (*Pierrot serviteur de la mort*), with Deburau's older son Paul playing the part originally written for his father.[7] The author of the pantomime was Champfleury, a young short-story writer who had already been praised by Victor Hugo.[8] Gustave Le Vavasseur, a school friend of Baudelaire's, remembered that the future author of *Les Fleurs du mal* was obsessed with the original Deburau, Jean-Gaspard-Baptiste, during his adolescence. Even then, Baudelaire haunted the Théâtre des Funambules.[9]

If Banville had claimed that Deburau's pantomimes, when seen one after another, were all episodes of a continuous poem, the same can be said of the *Petits poèmes en prose*. Each is like a scene from a single pantomime of the type known as *pantomime macabre*. Paris is the stage set on which Baudelaire's visions are being acted out. As the only member of the audience who is in on the secret, Baudelaire hides in the shadows of a world that has become a theater. It is impossible to tell whether the stories told in the prose poems are drawn from real life or merely staged for effect. Baudelaire keeps a straight face throughout, maintaining an icy sangfroid no matter how bizarre the scenario. A pantomime is "unnatural," to quote Champfleury's word; in contemporary terms, the artificiality of the pantomime could be compared to that of a silent film.[10] Gestures, bodily attitudes, and gazes are exaggerated so as to become visible to the furthest reaches of the audience. Pantomimes have no claim to realism or verisimilitude. Their plots are often illogical, the stage sets exaggeratedly artificial. One style of pantomime, called *pantomime féerique*, used magical tricks, sorcerers, and fairies. Pantomimes always rely on clichés (*poncifs*). Sadness, joy, and greed are signified by glaringly legible expressions. Paradoxically, pantomimes can also seem less artificial than spoken theater, because the corporeal language of the actor is understood with an immediacy and clarity that words, especially those spoken in alexandrine verse, rarely achieve. The aim of the pantomime is to reach, through exaggeration, condensation, and simplification, toward a more primitive truth.

In his essay on the comic, Baudelaire defines pantomime both as "the essence of comedy" and as "comedy stripped bare."[11] For Baudelaire, the effect of the comic is to awaken in us a satanic feeling of superiority: we laugh when we watch someone fall. But that which is comic from the spectator's point of view may very well be catastrophic for the victim. In the prose poems, the pantomimes recorded by Baudelaire are almost always violent; often, the violence edges into sadism. We do not know if we should consider this violence as a spectator at the Funambules would have (namely, as a feigned catastrophe meant to elicit laughter), or take it literally. In contrast, even if some of Jean-Gaspard-Baptiste Deburau's pantomimes featured displays of grotesque sadism (heads were cut off by Pierrot's sword, old men's wigs set on fire, children murdered in their sleep), everyone in the audience knew that these acts were not "for real."[12]

In some of Baudelaire's prose poems, the pantomime reaches a shrill intensity that approaches the violent humor of the Funambules. In "The Savage Woman and the Little Sweetheart," Baudelaire's putative stand-in finds a way to torture his mistress by regaling her with the story of a circus manager who pelts his wife with raw meat and beats her with a stick.[13] "That stick isn't the sort used in comedies," he hastens to add, "did you hear it resound on the flesh. . . . So now her eyes bulge from her head and she howls *more naturally*."[14] The mistress is supposed to believe that the story is true, and that the violence is not feigned: the beating on the stage of the funfair is "for real." Even when the plot of Baudelaire's pantomime is heroic, the spectacle is, again, sadistic. In "A Hero's Death," the longest of the prose poems, the clown and mime Fancioulle is at the center of a tragic tale.[15] He has plotted against the prince, his master, and has been sentenced to death. His last pantomime, on the very night his execution is supposed to take place, is a triumph. The narrator of the prose poem, who is one of the spectators in the audience, considers Fancioulle as the equal of the greatest artists. Although Baudelaire never describes the plot of Fancioulle's pantomime, we know that his "divine" and "supernatural" performance incites the audience to unexpected heights of pleasure. But Fancioulle's pantomime is interrupted by the trill of a whistle, and the mime falls dead on the stage. In the prose poem, the death of the mime is "for real," and the *pantomime macabre* is not a fiction.

Is Fancioulle's execution written as a pantomime, which the actor performs on the stage, or does the mime elude his execution by dying? Fancioulle's death is his final performance; but if the actor dies, what we see on stage cannot be considered a performance. A natural event prevents him from following the script. Death is the most real, and the least artificial, of all possible stories. In his treatise on the beautiful and the sublime, Burke says that, if an execution were scheduled at the same time as the performance of a tragedy, the theaters would empty out and the audience would flock to the spectacle of someone being put to death. No tragedy performed on the stage can be a match, in sheer entertainment value, for a real death. The moral of Baudelaire's story is either that art is powerless against death, or that art can defeat death, by making death into art. Either way, the desperate secret of the poem is the parody of a moral lesson. The only real event in the prose poem is not the pantomime itself, but the reaction that the pantomime inspires—the cacophonous mixture of admiration, compassion, and sadistic pleasure echoing in the hearts of those who witness the spectacle.

In "The Old Acrobat," a prose poem that was published with two other city pieces, "The Widows" and "The Crowds," in November 1861, Baudelaire is stunned by the spectacle of an old circus performer in a crowded funfair.[16] Dressed in rags, the destitute old man stands alone in front of his booth, incapable of ever attracting again an audience to whatever it is he still has to offer. (We are reminded of Kafka's "Hunger Artist": at the end of his career, the kind of spectacle at which he excelled is no longer of any interest at all.) The silence of the elderly acrobat contrasts with the joyous sounds of the fair—"hawkers' cries" blending with "thundering brass" and "exploding rockets":

> There was indeed a formidable rivalry among the booths; they squalled, bellowed, and howled. . . . He did not shout; he sang no song. . . . He stood silent and motionless. . . .
>
> But what a deep, unforgettable gaze he sent around the crowd and the lights, whose moving flood stopped a few steps away from his repulsive poverty![17]

No longer able to entertain the crowd with his acrobatic feats, the old man has now become the unwilling hero of a pantomime meant for the skilled eye of the spectator alone. We do not really see the old acrobat. We look through him, instead of at him. (Similarly, at the end of Kafka's story, the Hunger Artist has become invisible, even when he reaches, finally, the pinnacle of his art.) The miserable old man who despairs at his invisibility holds a distorted mirror to the "painter of modern life," compared by Baudelaire to "*a prince* who rejoices in his incognito."[18] Baudelaire and his reflected double are separated by layers of illusion, artifice, and irony. It is up to us to decide whether Baudelaire is engaged in an act of self-derision by making the old man an image of himself, or expressing true compassion.

To paint a portrait of the artist as a *saltimbanque* may have been shocking in the 1830s; but in 1861, when Baudelaire's poem was first published, the trope was well on its way to becoming a cliché. Baudelaire's incapacitated acrobat, unable to lift even a foot from the earth, both echoes and mocks the star-gazer of Banville and Gautier, who danced above the abyss.[19] When he contemplates the image of an immobilized acrobat, Baudelaire may be nostalgic for the bygone era of the pantomime at the Théâtre des Funambules, or he may be ridiculing the Romantic infatuation with tightrope walkers. In the prose poem's final image, the likeness between Baudelaire and the acrobat becomes explicit, and can be read as the punch line of a bitter joke:

> And as I went home, obsessed by this vision, I tried to analyze my sudden grief, and I said to myself: I have just seen the image of the old man of letters who has outlived the generation he so brilliantly amused; the image of the old poet who has no friends, no family, no children, degraded by his poverty and by public ingratitude, and into whose booth the forgetful world no longer wishes to enter![20]

The old man remains shrouded in his invisibility. Baudelaire does not see the acrobat; he sees himself looking at a desperate pantomime (or the absence of one) and creating a poetic image. Baudelaire is speaking to himself, and trying to understand his own suffering. No words are exchanged with the acrobat; no effort is made to reach out to him, to hear his story from him, or to alleviate his suffering. Even the idea of charity is dismissed, lest it humiliate both the giver and the receiver of it.[21] Just as the decrepit old acrobat is no longer performing his act, Baudelaire has stopped performing as an observer of the man's life. Baudelaire tricks the spectators into believing that they were looking at a lonesome old man at the funfair, while, all this time, the acrobat was in fact posing, as if he were a mirror, for a self-portrait of the person looking at him. It was all a trompe-l'oeil. In the vertiginous world of these poems, everything stands as an image of something else.

In the prose poems, the immobilized acrobat (like a poet incapable of writing verse) is not unique. Many other silent spectacles of degradation mirror the *pantomime macabre*. In "The Eyes of the Poor," we are faced not with one but with three such images of destitution—a father and his two young sons, all of them equally helpless. Baudelaire portrays himself sitting with his mistress inside a luxurious new café, situated "at the corner of a new boulevard." Brilliantly lit up by gaslight, the café is a triumphant spectacle in gold and white. The whiteness of the walls is "blinding"; the café's enormous mirrors scintillate and glitter. Standing on the sidewalk across from the café, the destitute man and his two sons are transfixed by the contemplation of this stunning trompe-l'oeil:

These three faces were extraordinarily serious, and their six eyes stared unblinkingly at the new café, all revealing the same degree of admiration. . . . The father's eyes said: "How beautiful it is! How beautiful! You'd say that all the gold of this sad world had gathered on these walls!" The eyes of the little boy: "How beautiful it is! How beautiful! But it's a house you can enter into only if you're not like us."[22]

Engaged both in mute contemplation and in silent monologues, the poor are locked up within the claustrophobic confines of themselves, and forever excluded from the glittering new world that the café represents. They are looking into our world, the world of poets, cafés, and the brilliant gaslights of "nightlife"; but we also are looking into theirs. Each is a spectacle for the other—a dismal entertainment. We look at one another from the outside, as distant images we can never touch, or be touched by.[23] In the Paris cafés, funfairs, and public gardens, Baudelaire comes across, as if by accident, a series of unscripted spectacles. But the people in them have no idea that they are playing a part. They are distorted mirrors in which Baudelaire contemplates his own face—silent echo chambers in which only his words resonate.

Machines of Vision

As Jules Laforgue so perceptively observed, Baudelaire was the first poet to speak of Paris from the perspective of a man living "in the daily hell of the capital" by bringing up such unpoetic subjects as gaslight, gambling parlors, funfairs, hospitals, and brothels.[24] The prose poems deliberately display the abjection of the city instead of hiding it. We see it in the image of the pathetic family standing transfixed in front of the modern café, in the trembling old man who begs for money in front of a tobacco shop, in the deranged prostitute who trolls for clients in the faubourg, and in the old woman behind her window. Baudelaire exposes the lives of "the weak, the ruined, the sad and the orphaned."[25] If some of the last vestiges of their humanity are manifested in a sense of shame, and the desire to keep the spectacle of their poverty to themselves, Baudelaire strips them even of this. We look at them through peepholes, and see the interiors in which the most impoverished Parisians live. Baudelaire even invites us into his own room, which he describes in all of its squalor: "Look at the stupid furniture, all dusty and beat up; the fireplace without a fire, without embers, spattered with saliva; the gloomy windows where the rain has licked furrows through the dust."[26] In the prose poem with which the collection ends, we follow the two dogs of a circus acrobat to the sad domicile of their owner. Baudelaire "lets us into the room of the absent circus acrobat," a hovel consisting in rickety chairs, soiled blankets, and broken musical instruments littering the floor.

But even these scenes of destitution, which carefully incorporate details apparently taken from real lives, are meant to deceive the reader. In the nineteenth century, many trompe-l'oeil paintings represented the leftovers of everyday life: scraps of paper, nutshells, or fruit peels, detritus so banal and so seemingly devoid of aesthetic interest that the spectator assumed that they were real, rather than the carefully chosen subject of a painting. Baudelaire's trompe-l'oeil shows us these "leftovers" of everyday Parisian life. Our attention is drawn to pitiful, insignificant objects; but we are also shown those people who, in nineteenth-century Paris, are the human equivalent of pitiful, insignificant objects. The beggars, prostitutes, and old women who are the subjects of these poems seem unworthy of being represented; and so we forget that what we are reading are poems, not images drawn from real life. These are people who, after all, should not be making an appearance in a poem. They belong in the prosaic world of a writer like Champfleury, whose short story "Chien-Caillou" tells the tale of a poor engraver and a streetwalker. Baudelaire praised the story for its realism and lack of artifice. More famously, he eulogized Hugo's *Les Misérables* as "a plea for the *destitute* (those who *suffer* from poverty and those who are *dishonored* by poverty)."[27] The people he chronicles in his own prose poems could have escaped from the teeming world of Hugo's melodrama.

But in contrast to Hugo, Baudelaire does not concern himself with the weak, the orphaned, and the destitute for their own sake. The little scenes of Parisian life he describes lead nowhere; they refuse to agglomerate into a larger picture, as they always do in the melodramas of Hugo. Baudelaire's characters emerge from obscurity, but their newly acquired visibility leaves almost nothing in its wake—certainly nothing as clear-cut as pity, or outrage at the sheer injustice of the world. When Hugo wrote *Les Misérables*, his explicit goal was to achieve political change by drawing attention to the social mechanisms that created real-life tragedies, such as the stories of Fantine and Cosette. Baudelaire, however, did not imagine that the kind of literature he wrote could change the world; and neither did he wish it to do so. In his intimate journals, he noted that "to be a useful citizen has always struck me as particularly distasteful."[28] Reflecting on his own participation in the Revolution of 1848, he remembers most of all his "intoxication." But he immediately attributes the thrill he felt when Paris took up arms against King Louis Philippe to a natural craving for vengeance and destruction. In "Let Us Beat Up the Poor," which is perhaps the most politically provocative of all his prose poems, he ridicules utopian political thinkers for their "elucubrations." In his view, radical social reformers like Fourier or Proudhon either wish to sentence the poor to the endless slavery of disciplined work, or they try to convince them that they are kings and queens in disguise. In both cases, social reformers are doomed to fail because they believe in the perfectibility of human nature, in work (as opposed to the aristocratic leisure), and in the regimented production of art. At the end of the poem, Baudelaire's stand-in beats an old beggar to a nearly lifeless pulp. The purpose of the beating is to teach the beggar all about equality and freedom. When the beggar finally fights back, he is praised effusively and given a generous sum of money. "Let Us Beat Up the Poor" was considered so profoundly offensive that it was rejected by all literary journals in Baudelaire's lifetime; and it is true that the sheer bitterness of the poem is difficult to stomach. It is impossible to conceive of the poem as an attempt to solve the problem of poverty, any more than we can imagine Swift's "Modest Proposal" as an attempt to "solve" the Irish problem by encouraging cannibalism.[29]

What we see in Baudelaire's prose poems, instead, is an image in trompe-l'oeil. We are repeatedly being led in the wrong direction; we are never looking at what we thought we were looking at.[30] The prose poems are so filled with pathetic and sordid details that they seem to be actively denying us the aesthetic pleasure derived from the reading of poetry. It is as if they had distanced themselves from the realm of the aesthetic in order to appear as stand-ins for the real world of nineteenth-century Paris. The poor in *Le Spleen de Paris* seem too real, as if they had intruded into the world of poetry (like the family that intrudes into the sight line of those who sit in the resplendent new café). But, at the same time, we are being deceived, because the real nineteenth-century Paris is being implacably shut out of the poems, as a world of hyperbolic artificiality takes its place.

In *Les Misérables*, Hugo moves us with the sufferings of the seamstress-turned-prostitute Fantine and her illegitimate child Cosette, reduced into slavery by the monstrous Thénardiers. The reader becomes a witness incapable of intervening and of relieving someone else's suffering. We are horrified when Fantine has her front teeth pulled out so she can pay for little Cosette's medicines. We suffer with Fantine, as if we were real-life witnesses to her larger-than-life agony. We do not feel the same

compassion for Baudelaire's panoply of beggars, old women, and destitute children. Hugo makes his characters larger than life so that we can
feel both pity and admiration for them. But we cannot picture Baudelaire's characters as flesh-and-blood creatures. The helplessness of those
who live inside Hugo's world becomes all the more unbearable for the
reader since it brings out the extremity of their courage: the lower they
fall in the eyes of society, the higher they rise on the scale of inherent
goodness and Christ-like suffering. In the *Petits poèmes en prose*, Baudelaire's characters are smaller than life. They are diminished, degraded;
they no longer even have a past, as if having one's own story were a luxury they could not afford, or as if each were too fragile an entity for a past
to adhere to. They no longer have the strength to carry the weight of
their memories with them. All the stories in *Les Misérables* form an immense chain of cause and effect; the decisions and actions of each character have momentous consequences on all the other characters. Each
of Baudelaire's prose poems is closed in on itself. The prose poems have
no room to expand, as if they were always looking at themselves instead
of looking outward. Just as each prose poem is trapped within itself, each
of the characters in the prose poems, in turn, is trapped inside a world of
pure artifice.

Baudelaire acknowledged Hugo's idealistic ambition when he called *Les
Misérables* "a book of compassion" (*un livre de charité*).[31] In private, however,
he confessed to his mother that he had found the book "nauseating" and
"inept" because of its overflowing sentimentality.[32] His prose poems are the
opposite of charitable. He referred to some of them as "horrors" and "monstrosities," going so far as to boast that they could provoke miscarriages in
pregnant women.[33] Two of these "monstrosities" were published under the
title "Little Poems of the Werewolf" ("Petits poèmes lycanthropes"). In a letter Baudelaire wrote to Hugo in 1859, he self-consciously perpetuates the
legend that he really was an unfeeling monster: "I live very comfortably with
shame branded on me (*sous ma flétrissure*), and I realize now that, whatever
genre of literature I shall choose to pour my feelings into, I will forever remain a monster and a werewolf."[34] Throughout the *Petits poèmes en prose*, this
"werewolf" nature manifests itself in physical assaults on the weakest sheep
of the human flock.

André Breton and Jean-Paul Sartre both came to the conclusion that
the sadistic outbursts in the prose poems contained Baudelaire's philosophy of life in a nutshell. In the provocative cruelty and dark humor of
Baudelaire, Breton found an inspiration for the surrealists' assault on

Christian morality, if not on rationality itself; while Sartre saw in these unprovoked and apparently inexplicable actions a manifestation of Baudelaire's desperate desire for a freedom without limits.[35] But the exaggerated sadism Baudelaire theatrically displays has nothing to do with freedom, whether his own or anyone else's. In these poems, Baudelaire mocks the sentimental view of the poor popularized by politically engaged writers such as Hugo, Eugène Suë, or George Sand—who inspired some of the most venomous pages in Baudelaire's journals, where she is repeatedly denounced for her prolixity and idealism.[36] Baudelaire's own position was far too precarious for him to publicly attack established authors like Victor Hugo. Instead, his vicious assaults grotesquely diminish the long-suffering martyrs that Hugo or Suë were renowned for creating. Whereas the suffering of Fantine is Christ-like in its power to redeem, the suffering of the characters in Baudelaire's poems is precisely not Christ-like. They suffer not like a God, but like an animal—a beast of burden whose agony is ultimately of no consequence. Their suffering redeems nothing, and will have never provided the opportunity for innocence to shine.

Walter Benjamin wrote that "The discovery of the mechanistic aspects of the human body is the characteristic trait of the sadist. One can say that the sadist tries to replace the human organism with the image of machinery."[37] Hugo makes us imagine fictional mechanisms as real bodies, but the sadist, as Benjamin argues, imagines real bodies as mere mechanisms. Baudelaire's fascination with trompe-l'oeil, optical tricks, and mechanistic images takes the place of any effort at representing real bodies and real suffering. Hugo believes that nature is good, and that the suffering of innocent victims like Cosette and Fantine must be blamed on the society they live in. Hell, for Hugo, is the opposite of the state of nature: it is made possible by the perversions of city life and human society. But nature itself is abhorrent to Baudelaire, who finds in artifice the sole source of beauty in the modern world. The *Petits poèmes en prose* trap the viewer inside a relentless mechanism, the purpose of which is to entertain us with willfully deceitful illusions. Baudelaire gives us spectacles in which any trace of the authentically human has been deliberately diminished.

No organic life-form is allowed to flourish in the Parisian prose poems. Instead, Baudelaire finds his delight in the inorganic, the artificial, and the disembodied. In "The Gallant Marksman," a man shooting for sport at a target range systematically misses his objective until he imagines that the doll he is aiming at is his wife. The doll is soon decapitated. Since the body of the doll is already lifeless, the sadism in "The Gallant Marksman" lies in the fact that the flesh-and-blood wife has been reduced to an artificial and miniaturized image of herself. This outrageous act does not, however, qualify as truly murderous. In *Les Misérables,* Hugo moves the readers to tears when he describes the rag doll to which little Cosette desperately clings. Here the doll is not an empty simulacrum of the child, but the sign of her victimization. This detail draws our attention to the pitifully small, doll-like body of Cosette. The doll in "The Gallant Marksman" serves the opposite purpose. Our attention is drawn away from real bodies and real suffering.

It seems incomprehensible, at first, that an aesthete like Baudelaire would have recourse to the crowd-pleasing trickery of trompe-l'oeil. The prose poems do not rise to the ethereal regions of the sublime, nor do they descend to the nether regions of realism. Instead, they unfold in a world of stand-ins and simulacra. The views of Paris are not drawn from life (in French, *d'après nature*). They are modeled on the kind of spectacular artifice that proved so irresistible to mid-nineteenth-century crowds. Baudelaire was renowned for his elitism and his hostility to progress; and yet he proclaimed that the superficial pleasures derived from optical tricks and trompe-l'oeil images were in fact the highest forms of artistic expression. Holding up a mirror to the modern Paris, he incorporated into his prose poetry the technologically advanced but aesthetically primitive modes of visual entertainment that seemed so incompatible with the kind of higher aesthetic experience he had previously tried to conjure in his verse poems.

In a brief essay on childhood, Baudelaire described a popular optical device, the phenakisticope, with obsessive precision. He dismissed the phenakisticope as nothing more than "a scientific toy." (Like a magic lantern, the phenakisticope created the cinematic illusion of movement from two revolving discs on which miniature figures had been painted.) But Baudelaire also confessed that these toylike objects marked our own initiation into the realm of art. "All children talk to their toys: toys become actors in the great drama of life, miniaturized in the dark rooms of their little brains."[38] Later, while he was writing the dedication of the *Petits poèmes en prose,* Baudelaire noted that his collection of prose poems was structured so as to resemble "a spiral on a screw or a kaleidoscope."[39] The artist Constantin Guys, drifting through the streets and boulevards of Paris, like Baudelaire, was famously compared, in "The Painter of Modern Life," to "a kaleidoscope endowed with consciousness which, with each of his moves, captures life's multiplicity and the shifting grace of all the aspects of life."[40]

In English, a diorama is a three-dimensional scene, either life-size or miniaturized, in which figures are set against a naturalistic background. In Baudelaire's lifetime, however, the word referred to the rotunda-shaped building built by Daguerre on the Boulevard du Temple. Daguerre's diorama, which opened to the public in 1822, had, mounted on its walls, huge curved panels depicting celebrated historical episodes and views of famous cities. While the spectators rotated on a semicircular platform, the paintings were illuminated through an intricate manipulation of the natural light filtering through the tall windows and skylights so as to create the lifelike illusion of movement.[41] In the "Salon of 1859," Baudelaire claimed that Daguerre's diorama gave him more pleasure than landscape paintings: "I wish to be taken back to the dioramas, the brutal and enormous magic of which forces its useful illusion on me. I prefer to look at these stage sets, where I find, artistically expressed and tragically condensed, my most precious dreams."[42] Almost every word of the description is meant to provoke. What purpose could a diorama possibly serve, besides satisfying a widespread craving for empty entertainment? How could the universally popular diorama, which created its visual deception through figurative painting and tricks of stage lighting, have condensed Baudelaire's "most precious dreams"?[43]

The diorama was more primitive than both figurative art and the theater, the two genres from which it derived its existence. Compared with landscape paintings, the images offered to the public by Daguerre were of little artistic value. A view of Napoleon's tomb in Saint Helena would follow the interior of the Cathedral of Canterbury, a representation of the Deluge would succeed a view of Paris seen from Montmartre. These images were not selected for their originality, but, on the contrary, because most spectators were already all too familiar with them. There were no Delacroix or Courbets among the painters of dioramas.[44] The sensation of seeing an image move was enhanced by the pleasure of recognizing a well-known view. Around 1835, Daguerre invented the even more spectacular *diorama à double effet*, a mechanism that projected light onto a painting to re-create different moments of the day. A translucent panel was painted on both sides, and illuminated from the front, then from the back. The spectators saw, for example, an image of the empty church of Saint-Étienne-du-Mont in the daytime, which progressively transformed itself into a candlelit view of the crowded church during the midnight mass. A journalist who attended the opening session of Da-

guerre's double diorama described it as "a succession of fleeting and immaterial illusions" (*une succession d'illusions rapides et indéfinissables*).[45]
Two illusions followed each other before the eyes of the confused view-
ers. Removed from the natural cycle of day and night, they saw a world
shaped by artificial light.

What Baudelaire's prose poems aim to show is precisely this disorienting moment of transformation. Many of them take place at twilight,
like a *diorama à double effet*. In the poem "The Double Bedroom" ("La
chambre double"), the soft, dreamlike pinks and blues of an ideal vision
illuminate Baudelaire's room at first. But once the image of a cramped,
dirty, and desolate interior has been superimposed on this initial image,
the room is lit up by the harsh gray light of Paris. The unexpected shift
from one vision to the next operates exactly as the double diorama did.
In "The Savage Woman and the Little Sweetheart," the vision of a primitive human animal displayed in a cage and fed slices of raw meat follows
an evocation of Baudelaire's spoiled mistress, who enjoys the finest foods
and the most subtle perfumes. The female quasi-human at the funfair is
so evidently a grotesque fantasy that the image of the "little sweetheart"
appears, in retrospect, equally unreal. One scene is impossibly dark, the
other impossibly light. In the poem entitled "Which Is the Real Benedicta?" the beloved woman, so ravishing and ethereal in her lifetime, is
transformed after her death into a "bizarre" and "hysterical" creature
who claims to be the "real" Benedicta. A grotesquely dark vision succeeds
a clichéd image of perfection. The poem is a parodic reenactment of the
morbid tales of Poe, such as "Ligeia" or "Berenice," which Baudelaire
had himself translated.[46] The poem "A Thoroughbred Horse," which follows "Which Is the Real Benedicta?" in Baudelaire's collection, juxta-
poses two radically opposed descriptions of an aging woman: "She is
truly ugly. And yet she is lovely! . . . She is an ant, a spider, if you wish;
even a skeleton; but she is also a drink, a potion, sorcery! In a word, exquisite."[47] A relentless satire of Romantic ideals of the feminine culmi-
nates in the debasement of vision itself. The freshly dug grave of Benedicta, in which her lover's leg becomes caught, is "the grave of the ideal."
In the degraded world of Baudelaire's prose poems, it is impossible to
see an image of beauty that does not transform, moments later, into a
nightmarish vision; and, conversely, it is impossible to witness a horrific
vision that does not have its own very special kind of beauty.[48]

As in a diorama, the observer in the prose poems is so thoroughly removed from the natural world that he loses all sense of proportion. In
Le Spleen de Paris, vision becomes the most unnatural of all the senses.

Objects and figures can no longer be measured in relation to one another. The spectator of a diorama is both consuming images and being consumed by them: dwarfed by the panels that surround us, we are overwhelmed by the sheer size of the images. Similarly, for the flaneur in the prose poems, distances are blurred, scale is distorted, and images fold the real into the chimerical. Baudelaire is watching images of Parisian life, but he also stands inside these images, a minuscule actor on the huge stage-set of Paris, looking at the mute phantasmagoria of modern life. We do not see a real body moving from place to place. Instead, we find the observer on a newly built boulevard, in the café, or in front of the tobacco shop, as if he had been magically transported from one stage set to another. The flaneur is everywhere and nowhere at the same time.

One could invoke, however anachronistically, Baudelaire's "cubism," or his "cubist dioramas." In "The Widows," he shifts and reassembles the scattered pieces of old women so as to create a generic portrait. In the real world, it would be impossible to see all of these pieces at once in a single glance. Baudelaire artificially unifies different moments into one vision. The prose poem entitled "The Windows" shows an old woman inside her tiny room. We see her in detail through the glass, so close that we could almost touch her. But she is also said to live somewhere far "beyond waves and waves of roofs." She is both unrealistically close and impossibly distant, as if she were being observed through an optical device that magnifies distant objects into an illusory proximity. In a painting, the old woman would be a detail in a corner; but here the detail occupies the center of the image. As a consequence, everything is out of scale. The old woman should be a spectator in a painting representing something more significant than herself. She will never be aware that the painting is one she posed for.

In the prose poem entitled "The Projects," a flaneur drifting through the streets of Paris acts out, in the "dark room" of his mind, little scenes in which his mistress finds herself, successively, inside a medieval castle, a tropical jungle, and an inn. What the flaneur sees is a mechanism through which images are produced, multiplied, and derealized. He is not looking at the real Paris. The woman in the jungle is inspired by an engraving seen in the display window of a printer's shop. A detail in an engraving, the woman is transported into a world of sheer artifice. As her likeness is mechanically conjured in different places, she is no longer herself, a flesh-and-blood person. She becomes a miniature image of who she would be, if only she were real.

Obscene Images: Photography and the Death of Art

The proliferation of images in Baudelaire's prose poems is not simply an unfurling phantasmagoria of visions. The process running rampant in the poems is the translation of everything into an image. The *Petits poèmes en prose* are a reflection of their times. What these times reflected, in turn, was a generalized obsession with the mechanical creation of illusions. It is a commonplace that photography, in the course of the nineteenth century, had a profound effect on the art of painting. Once a "perfect" likeness became the aftereffect of a mechanism, the creation of likenesses could no longer be an end in itself. But it has less often been noticed that photography came to fundamentally alter literature as well.

Like visual art, literary art does not only reproduce an image of who we are. Homeric poems do not simply record Homeric men and their heroic actions: Homeric men are themselves created by Homeric poems. When these poems are no longer read—when they are no longer taken seriously as the most perfect expression of who we once were, and of who we must strive to be—then Homeric men cease to exist. As photography became more and more triumphant, usurping the traditional place of the other arts, we inevitably began to imagine ourselves as an image of what we saw. A mechanism producing a miniature likeness replaced the painstaking re-creation of the most significant among us (the heroic, the aristocratic), color by color, stroke by stroke, into a larger-than-life image. For the first time, vast numbers of people could look at an image of themselves. But these "democratic vistas" were disappointingly small—a daguerreotype fits into the palm of a hand. Tiny ex-votos took the place of the most glorious manifestations of the painter's art. Daguerre's crowning technological achievement diminished our existence precisely because of our wish to immortalize ourselves. Too many people became immortal: Elysium was overcrowded.

For Baudelaire, photography was like the immortality it bought: a parody of art, just as the image of a staring, open-eyed face in a daguerreotype was a parody of eternal life. But the pervasiveness of these images, which was the natural consequence of our insatiable desire for them, became the surest sign of the "truth" of his prose poems. The parodic nature of these poems is a faithful reflection of the brave new world invented by Daguerre. Baudelaire, too, offered a faithful mirror to the desires of the Parisian crowds. He watched in horror as the crowds became infatuated with the promise of their own immortality. He described a situation in which "A madness, an extraordinary fanaticism overwhelmed all these new sun-worshippers. Strange abominations took place."[49] According to Baudelaire, the proliferation of pornographic images was one of these abominations. But the obscenity of photography was not only exemplified by the public's craving for pornographic images. Photography was obscene because the crowds that rushed to immortalize themselves in the silver sheen of daguerreotypes, "like one Narcissus," had become enraptured with the spectral image of themselves.

The Baudelaire of the prose poems is not a new Ovid telling the story of a collective Narcissus. Poetry is no longer something that exists inside the world, a book we could pick up in our hand, with the word *Metamorphoses* on its cover. We are, instead, inside the poem, as if trapped there—lured into an abyssal world where our image exerts a fascination that is impossible to resist. Baudelaire is simply a witness to the fact that everyone in the crowd has fallen into a photographic world of empty images. In Baudelaire's eyes, a photographer does nothing more than intervene in a mechanical process. He initiates and ends a technical procedure, but there is no act of creation. In the same sense, Baudelaire watches and interposes himself in the prose poems, but he does not create. He frames images from "real life." But "real life" has become nothing more than a headlong rush into images, and away from art.

It is not by chance that the only noble character in Baudelaire's prose poems, a tall and beautiful widow, is compared—in spite of her abject poverty—to a portrait in "these collections of aristocratic beauties of the past."[50] In the modern world of the prose poems, the widow appears out of place. She belongs to an aristocratic past, now hopelessly outmoded, in which the human face, painstakingly depicted in a portrait, reflected the innate nobility of the subject. Watched from a distance, as if by a contemplative voyeur, the beautiful widow is diametrically opposed to another female figure, the prostitute nicknamed "Miss Scalpel" (Mademoiselle Bistouri). The prostitute's grotesque pseudonym by itself is a sufficient sign of the monstrosity of the Paris she exemplifies. The story is both simple and perverse. After soliciting her client, Miss Scalpel takes him back to her squalid room, where she keeps a collection of photographic portraits of surgeons. Her fantasy is that they will make love to her while dressed in their white smocks still spattered with blood. Her life is not lived in a world she shares with anyone, least of all her clients; she experiences her inner life only through the photographic images she collects. Those images are the instruments of a sexual ritual that her customers are then forced to witness. Just as she has no real name, only a pseudonym by which she is known from the outside, she has no real past, or at least no past that is accessible either to her or to us. When asked about the origin of her bizarre fixation, she answers sadly, averting her gaze: "I do not know . . . I cannot remember" (*Je ne sais pas . . . je ne me souviens pas*).[51] Despite her obsession with spilled blood and wounded flesh, she is the exact opposite of a flesh-and-blood creature. She is a quasi-human machine, the function of which is to mechanically repeat the same story while obsessively looking at the same photographs (If Baudelaire were Dante, it is easy to imagine that Miss Scalpel would still be looking at the same images, and telling the same stories, to her customers in the afterlife.)

Miss Scalpel is a stand-in, in the eyes of Baudelaire, for the mid-nineteenth-century Parisian public as whole; she has become a mechanism for manipulating images and being manipulated by them. Having carefully selected moments from a fallen world, Baudelaire is fascinated by the images he chooses to exhibit, and so he shows them to us, again and again. This is what makes Miss Scalpel, ultimately, a stand-in for Baudelaire himself. He is fascinated by Miss Scalpel's fascination; he is repulsed both by her fascination and by his own. Instead of art, the public craves an image of its own degradation. This is what Baudelaire gives us: stories that have neither beginning nor end, except for those that chance imposes. At the end of his life, Baudelaire had deliberately stopped writing alexandrine verse so as to compose "poetry" in prose—*Le Spleen de Paris*. But the "poetry" he had decided to write was not only in prose. It was also perilously close to being not "written" at all, but simply recorded, in the same sense as a camera writes an image of the world in black and white.

In "The Counterfeit Coin," Baudelaire describes someone who "robs" a beggar by giving him a coin he knows to be counterfeit. An act that seems charitable turns out to be nothing more than the perverse image of a charitable act. There is a counterfeit act of charity: a kindness that appears real is in fact only an image. The image is not a faded version of the original: on the contrary, the image is a deliberate turning of the original on its head. It is not an act of charity to knowingly pass off a counterfeit coin on a beggar. It is, instead, a willful act of perversity, the purpose of which is not only to appear charitable in the eyes of others, but to mock the very idea of charity. Baudelaire unveils the alchemical process by which the appearance of charity in the eyes of others—which is a real value, a precious commodity—is bought with worthless money. The corrosive irony of the act lies not only inside the events narrated in the prose poem, but in the fact that the story it relates is real. In his essay "The Pagan School"—the very same essay from which Whitman extracted a quote to support his argument in favor of ordinary poetic sub-jects—Baudelaire freely confesses that someone told him the anecdote, and that he invented nothing.[52] His "poem" in prose is simply the selec-tion, framing, and careful reproduction of a reality that already exists. The poem itself is a counterfeit. There is no alexandrine verse, no in-vention, no charity, and almost no hope.

In another prose poem, "The Dog and the Perfume Bottle," Baude-laire presents the dismayed reader with a picture of someone offering a bottle of precious perfume to a dog, only to discover that the dog would have been far more pleased by the scent of excrement. The public, says Baudelaire, is this dog.[53] The black ribbon wrapped around the neck of Manet's "Olympia" only makes her more naked. Similarly, the veil of al-legory in this poem is so transparent as to be laughable—a vestige of clothing veiling a body's nudity increases its obscenity instead of lessen-ing it. What Baudelaire says, directly, indirectly, and in every other way, is obscene. If it were possible to speak yet more directly than in the allegory of the dog and the perfume, Baudelaire writes in his journals: "When it comes to literature, the French are scatophagous (*le Français est scatophage*). They lust after shit."[54] The sentiment expressed in the "poem" is perilously close to the actual opinion of Baudelaire, just as the anecdote Baudelaire hears about counterfeit acts of charity is perilously close to the "poem" entitled "The Counterfeit Coin." The suspicion lingers that even Miss Scalpel is not invented, and that—in the prose poem, at least—she is not only not a "poetic" creation, but that neither is she, in any sense, a "creation" at all. She and her gallery of bearded mas-culinity seem horrifyingly real. The fact that there is no story behind her, no explanation and no resolution, makes her life into an image of what a photograph gives us.

What Baudelaire offers to the public, what he throws in front of its collective snout, is an art that is not an art, a poetry that is not poetry, and a literature that is impossible to imagine as a fiction. The simple fact that the prose poems exist is an indictment of the public they were carefully crafted for. Baudelaire's systematic creation of poems in prose is not a confession that he had become unable to create alexandrine verse, but an accusation directed at the crowds who no longer want art. In a final irony, which would have been, in Baudelaire's eyes, both pitiful and comedic, the public's "lust" for the prose poems was minimal. Posterity's attitude toward them is not that they were a repudiation of the modern era and of its "scatophagous" tastes, but that they were uncannily and prophetically modern.

In his Belgian notes, Baudelaire summarized a prose poem entitled "A Future Phenomenon," which had been shown to him by one of his friends. Though this fact is not noted by Baudelaire, the author was the twenty-one-year-old Stéphane Mallarmé. Baudelaire was struck by the conceit: "The world has come to an end. A Barnum of the future shows to the degraded men of his time a beautiful woman of bygone ages, artificially preserved. 'What!' they say, can it be possible that human beings were once as beautiful as this?'" In Baudelaire's view, the young author's prose poem was insufficiently pessimistic. Baudelaire had a vision of the future that was far more catastrophic. He adds in his notes: "This is not true. The degraded man would admire himself and call beauty ugliness. See the deplorable Belgians."[55] As youthful admirers of Baudelaire, like Stéphane Mallarmé, Paul Verlaine, and Arthur Rimbaud, were obsessively looking for their own definitions of beauty, Baudelaire saw only P. T. Barnum and an "Americanized" future in which beauty, by whatever definition, was not merely a subject of indifference, but an actively repellent quality.

In the same set of notes, Baudelaire records twice a popular attraction at a funfair. The entry does not form a poem in prose; neither is it the draft of a future prose poem. It is the logical end of a process that led him from verse to prose. He simply records the true story of a spectacle in a neutral voice long since familiar to his readers, since it is the voice with which he wrote *Le Spleen de Paris*. While Goya gave us an allegorical vision of Saturn eating his own children, Baudelaire gives us the image of a man eating a live dog at a circus in Brussels: "A dog eaten alive for 20 francs," the audience (*le public*) composed "of women and children."[56] This obscene image comes from a circus. But the act of memorializing the spectacle for all of posterity is barely less obscene. This is where the prose poems lead—to an image of an absolute modernity and the hint of a future yet to come.

Conclusion

In Search of Lost Time

THE MODERN CITY, for Whitman and for Baudelaire, was not simply a place to live in, to look at, and to record. In a deeper and more essential sense, each city was a mechanism for living time in a certain way. Even as he was composing his obsessively detailed catalogs of city life, Whitman was not trying to paint a cityscape of New York; Baudelaire's prose poems show little interest either in the topography of Paris or in the minutiae of Parisian life. Very few concrete images of the city emerge against these receding backgrounds. Writing in Paris in the 1940s, the critic Georges Blin spoke of the all too familiar grayish chiaroscuro in which Baudelaire's prose poems seem to be bathed. Whitman's poems, too, are mostly colorless. What Paris or New York looked like, for Baudelaire and Whitman, was not important. What really mattered to them was how the modern city transformed the experience of time. Both Baudelaire and Whitman attempted, desperately and repeatedly, to capture the lineaments of that transformation.

In late-nineteenth-century New York and Paris, the leisurely pace of the flaneur was progressively becoming a thing of the past as time rushed headlong into its own future. As Georges Blin was meditating on Baudelaire's gray skies from the Paris of the Occupation, the architectural critic Siegfried Giedion was enthusiastically making a case for Haussmann's prescience. In his classic study *Space, Time, and Architecture,* Giedion noted that Haussmann took extraordinary steps, far in advance of his era, toward the solution of the traffic problem that would later be created by automobiles. "His critics, taking the scale of the *promeneur* as final, could not have been expected to understand such arrangements,

99

intended as they were for generations yet unborn," Giedion explains. "They could not have foreseen that these roads, carried clear over the horizon, would be the most 'productive' of the Prefect's 'expenditures,' and would constitute the future living space of Paris."[1] One of Haussmann's fiercest opponents, Adolphe Thiers, once remarked that people out walking from the Madeleine to the Place de l'Étoile will take several turns up and down the street to make their walks more enjoyable.[2] The idea that *flânerie* should shape the design of a city made no sense to Haussmann, who viewed urban planning as a way of finding the shortest route from one point to another. Having been pitched to the accelerated pace of urban transformation, expansion, and metamorphosis, urban time (or so it seemed) could no longer reclaim its original pace or its immemorial nature. In Baudelaire's prose poems, the time is never right. The repudiation of the past in Haussmann's forward-looking city has thrown everything—Baudelaire, Paris, and poetry—off-balance. The city is losing its memory, and Baudelaire is losing his capacity to memorialize the past as he is nearing his own end.

Both Baudelaire and Paris seem to be reaching the end of the line. The poems in prose, the last he ever wrote, should have been his testament. Had everything not been thrown off-balance, they should have been the legacy of a life—the past carrying over, seamlessly, poetically, and musically, into the present and the future. The prose poems, then, would have been a gift to future generations. Instead, the poems are trapped in a present moment that never seems to move either forward or backward. The "spleen of Paris" is the melancholy of a present that has been stripped of anticipation, of hope, and of memory. Neither the decrepit acrobat at the funfair, the old woman behind her window, or the "innocent monster" called Miss Scalpel has any right either to a past or to a future. What happened to them before, and what the future now holds in store for them, is beside the point. There is nothing left for them on either side of time. They are bereft of any kind of temporality except for a present moment that never ends, and that will never lead to any other time.

At the end of "Miss Scalpel," Baudelaire asks God why such bizarre creatures as Miss Scalpel exist: "Oh Creator! Can there be monsters in the eyes of God, who alone knows why they exist, how they *made themselves,* and how they could have *not made themselves?*"[3] Miss Scalpel could have never been born; she could have never "made herself." As if she had only been born as "Miss Scalpel," the name she received at birth is gone. The attraction Miss Scalpel feels toward blood-spattered surgeons re-

Charles Marville, Construction of Boulevard Henri-IV in Paris. View from the south with the Dome of the Pantheon in the background. Ca. 1870. Adoc-photos / ArtResource, NY

mains both mysterious, in the sense of being inexplicable, and monstrous, in the sense that we can imagine all too well the scenario at the origin of her obsession. Similarly, Baudelaire makes no attempt to explain the sadistic acts that have victimized the "bad glazier": "Besides, it would be impossible for me to say why this poor man aroused in me a hatred as sudden as it was overwhelming."[4] The hyperbolic hatred for the poor man and the sexual perversion of Miss Scalpel are both unaccounted for. They create events, and cause a story to be written, but the story's inner logic is a challenge to logic. What takes place inside the poems is of another order.

In most of the prose poems, hypotheses and guesses abound, pointing to enigmas that remain obstinately unsolved. At the end of "The Widows," Baudelaire wonders why the tall and noble widow is standing behind the barriers that separate the paying public of an outdoor concert from the "crowd of pariahs" too poor to afford a ticket:

> What an extraordinary sight! It cannot be, I said to myself, that her poverty, if indeed it is poverty, would admit of sordid penny-pinching.

Such a noble face assures me of it. So why does she remain, of her own free will, in surroundings where she is obviously out of place? But as I walked curiously past her, I believed I could guess the reason. The tall widow held by the hand a child who was dressed in black as she herself was; however low the entrance price, that money may well have been enough to pay for one of the little being's needs, or better still for a luxury, a toy.[5]

I believed I could guess the reason, that money may well have been enough: in this silent encounter, Baudelaire imagines what the reasons could be, and invents fictions to account for the behavior of the tall widow. But all these reasons are hypothetical: nothing in the text vouches for their truthfulness. We are projected inside a fiction that seems to be writing itself, just as Miss Scalpel is said to have "made herself." The legend of the tall widow is improvised before our eyes, as new hypotheses are being added. Writing the story of the widow becomes the spectacle of writing the story of the widow. The only "real" thing in the prose poem is the time of writing—the time it takes to read a gesture or an attitude; the time it takes for the act of writing to present itself as a spectacle. All that really happens is that someone imagines the legends he will add to a silent image.

In "The Counterfeit Coin," an anecdotal encounter in the city provides Baudelaire with another opportunity to improvise multiple fictions played out for himself only. After his friend gives a fake coin to a beggar, Baudelaire speculates on the possible causes and effects of such a gift:

Into my wretched brain, which is always trying to complicate matters . . . there suddenly came the idea that such behavior, on the part of my friend, could be excused only by a desire to create an event (*le désir de créer un événement*) in the poor devil's life, perhaps even to discover the diverse consequences, be they disastrous or otherwise, that can result from the presence of a counterfeit coin in the hands of a beggar. Could it not multiply in the form of real coins? Could it not also lead him to prison? An inn-keeper or a baker, for instance, would perhaps have him arrested either for making or passing counterfeit coins. But it was equally likely that the false coin could provide a poor little speculator with the seeds of a few days' riches. And so my imagination wandered along, lending wings to my friend's mind and drawing all possible deductions from all possible hypotheses.[6]

The desire to create a story, and so to cause something to happen, causes the poem, in turn, to speculate endlessly on what could possibly happen.

In his discussion of "The Counterfeit Coin," the late Jacques Derrida points out that the poem is centered on a proliferation, both monetary and intellectual, that obliterates the event at its origin:

> The event . . . takes the form of a meditation *on the event* and a meditation that is not exempt from reasoning and speculation—*ad infinitum.* The narrator speculates on speculation, on this event which, consisting in a gift (the gift of some money that proves, if one can put it that way, to be counterfeit), could well be the effect of a speculation that engenders, in turn, in a capitalistic fashion, other speculative events.[7]

A counterfeit coin causes endless speculation: it creates a multiplicity of hypothetical stories, just as it could, fictively speaking, create "real" money, or bring ephemeral wealth to a poor little speculator. The friend's odd behavior is diagnosed as a desire for experience—the desire to create an experience in someone else's life. Then Baudelaire imagines the results of this experience, which is also an experiment that acts out many imaginary "scenes" in an intellectual dumb-show: the scene at the baker's, the scene at the innkeeper's, the scene of a small- time speculator getting rich . . . It is as if the poem were nothing other than the container of other future, and still unwritten, poems. The "real" story recounted in "The Counterfeit Coin," which is the story of a fake coin given to a beggar, is upstaged by all the fictions invented by the narrator. The tobacco shop before which the actual incident occurs vanishes, to be quickly replaced by fictive backgrounds, such as the inn or the baker's shop. Modernity is not simply exemplified in the prosaic banality of a Parisian tobacco shop. For Baudelaire, modernity becomes the process through which time can be endlessly erased and written over. Time is not a still, homogeneous surface: it can be displaced and shifted around, as one would shift the backdrop of a play. The prose poems give us glimpses of other worlds, in which other stories, and other poems, could be writing themselves.

Derrida notes that "One generally thinks that narrative discourse reports events that have taken place outside it and before it. Narrative relation, so one thinks, does not report itself."[8] Instead, in Baudelaire's prose poems, the stories look as if they were telling themselves instead of telling past events. The poetic story presents itself as a kaleidoscopic display of fictive stories within the "real" story. Each of the lives glimpsed in the poems reproduces, as Baudelaire said of Constantin Guys, "life's multiplicity and the shifting grace of all life's aspects."[9] The raw and primitive magic conjured by Baudelaire erases the time of storytelling—which is to say, the past—in the spectacle of writing. The ecstasy experienced in the crowds (*l'ivresse des foules*) is a temporal ecstasy. Time can be "speculated upon," instead of following an ineluctable course toward death. In the lyric alexandrines of *Les Fleurs du mal,* Baudelaire is haunted by memory. But in *Le Spleen de Paris,* he literally tries to do away with time. "To *kill* Time (tuer *le Temps*). Isn't killing that monster everyone's most commonplace and most legitimate occupation?"[10] The monster of time has already been killed in modern Paris; and the broken-down poems in prose simply retell the story of its disappearance.

Whitman's obsession with time in the modern city is as radically modern as Baudelaire's; however, it takes on a very different form. Throughout *Leaves of Grass,* Whitman deliberately pictures time as a continuum instead of a process of endless fragmentation. Many critics have pointed to Whitman's manipulation of verb tenses. His frequent use of present participles tends to situate his poems in an eternal present: "Starting from fish-shape Paumanok where I was born," "Through Mannahatta's streets I walking, these things gathering," "Day upon day and year upon year, O city walking your streets."[11] By telling themselves in the present, the poems seem to be reflecting the self-enclosed world of the moment instead of narrating a past event. This is especially true of Whitman's city poems, which capture the spontaneity of life on the streets, exactly as a series of photographs would juxtapose views of one place at different moments in time, creating a temporal panorama masquerading as a spatial one. But placing each moment into an everlasting present is the opposite of telling a story. A narrative requires a beginning, a middle, and an end. With Whitman, we are always in the middle of an event. No narrative unfolds because we cannot emerge from an endlessly expanding present. With each new line, something begins again, but nothing ever comes to an end. It as if the poem could go on forever. The present engulfs everything else, leaving room for neither the past nor the future.

Refusing to emerge from a beginning or toward an end, Whitman endlessly retraces his steps. In his poems and his personal recollections, he recounts, over and over again, his practice of going for strolls on Broadway or on the Bowery, sitting next to the omnibus driver, gazing at the crowds on the streets, and merging into them. But very little actually happens. Much of his journalism also is remarkably devoid of narrative intent, to the point of being, from a contemporary perspective, almost unreadable. A piece appropriately entitled "A Lazy Day," which records a walk down the Battery and an encounter with a group of street urchins, concludes with this puzzling statement: "For the next two or three hours, we possess no recollection of having done anything in particular."[12] As the story of an ordinary day in New York comes to a close, Whitman's voice goes utterly blank. Watching the "mighty rush of men, business, carts, carriages, and clang" on Broadway, Whitman identifies himself as "one of the citizens." There is nothing more to him than that.[13] Because he is so thoroughly and willfully immersed in an everlasting present, nothing can happen to him. He is a storyteller without a story.

Although largely based on anecdotes and real-life experiences, Whitman's poetry of New York is bereft of actual events. The present overwhelms everything, like a cataclysmic flood; yet at the same time nothing happens in the present. Instead of speaking with strangers on the streets, Whitman speculates about an imaginary past life shared with them and about the increasingly remote possibility of another encounter in the future. The present consists in remembering a past that never happened and imagining stories that will never take place. Nothing can happen because the present never leads outside of itself. Whitman's city poems sometimes hint at individual stories, but they never unfurl into the flesh and blood of particularity. Just like the Paris of Baudelaire's *Petits poèmes en prose,* his New York evokes an atmosphere while effacing the specifics of people's lives. Whitman portrayed many city types in *Leaves of Grass:* the fireman, the omnibus driver, the businessman, the emigrant, the opium addict, the prostitute. He even famously categorized himself as another stereotype of New York life, the "loafer." But none of these types ever appear as anything but clichés. Their stories never have a chance to evolve in time. Only the present counts, since the present moment is the time when, however briefly, these figures become visible to Whitman.

In one of his most Baudelairian poems, "The City Dead-House," Whitman describes the unclaimed body of a prostitute, who has apparently committed suicide. The poem unfolds entirely in the present. The past and the future are set aside, as if these other and more alien kinds of time could not possibly have any meaning:

> By the city dead-house by the gate,
> As idly sauntering wending my way from the clangor,
> I curious pause, for lo, an outcast form, a poor dead prostitute
> brought,
> Her corpse they deposit unclaim'd, it lies on the damp brick
> pavement,
> The divine woman, her body, I see the body, I look on it alone,

The house once full of passion and beauty, all else I notice not,
. . . .
Unclaim'd, avoided house—take one breath from my tremulous
    lips,
Take one tear dropt aside as I go for thought of you.[14]

The faceless and anonymous woman has lost not only her future, but also her past. Whom her lips have kissed before, why, or how, is beside the point. It is as if she had never been a prostitute, but had always been—as she is, now, in the eyes looking at her—a "divine woman." In the past, her body was "full of life and passion," instead of being degraded by hunger, poverty, and the desires of others. The story is of the present moment of Whitman's kiss. No other time is real, either for him or for the poem. The suicide has no ability to tell her own story, and Whitman has no wish to tell it. The woman is dead, and so nothing further will ever happen to her again. The whole poem makes it seem as if she had never lived at all.

In "The City Dead-House," the present is the dead end of time. It leads, cyclically, into itself. Whitman stops in the course of his walk to look at the dead woman, then goes away in search of other things to look at, fantasize upon, and write poems about. The dead woman was never more than a brief pause in his never-ending perambulation around Manhattan and Brooklyn. His place in time is not a place, but a perpetual wandering—a purposeful evasion of both the past and the future. Whitman and Baudelaire can be pictured as having fallen into a peculiar form of present time from which they will not, or cannot, emerge. More than anything, they wanted to be attuned to the rhythm of the present, transmuting its qualities into sound, words, sentences, and images. That neither of these projects could ever be completed is evidence of the necessarily unending and unfinished quality of the present and of urban time.

In his *Confessions*, Augustine explains that our experience of time can be divided into three kinds. "There are three times," Augustine argues, "a present of past things, a present of present things, and a present of future" (*Tempora sunt tria, praesens de praeteritis, praesens de praesentibus, praesens de futuris*). "The present of past things," says Augustine, "is memory (*memoria*); the present of present things is direct perception (*contuitus*); and the present of future things is expectation (*expectatio*)."[15] If epic poetry systematically remembers the past of a people, and so carries it forth into the living present, then lyric poetry, in the same sense, makes vividly present the individual past. But the experience of the present time in the present is an activity that came to characterize, in many ways, the radically modern poetry of the mid-nineteenth century. By letting go of the past, and cleaving closely to the spectacle of Parisian streets, Baudelaire, at the end of his life, is no longer a lyric poet, as he was in *Les Fleurs du mal*.[16] The past is not carried forth into the present, as it is done collectively in epic poetry, and individually in lyric. In the prose poems, Paris is not a site of memorialization. The past, now, is no longer an issue. What Baudelaire wishes to bring into the present is simply the present. He wants to experience and express "the present of present things"; and what becomes increasingly vivid is an ever-increasing sense of emptiness and temporal void.

Whitman, on the other hand, narrates a time shot through with vestiges of the past. But these vestiges are impossible to fully grasp or articulate. The past appears not as meaningful words but as shards of sound—sonic elements from a pre-European America that cannot be made fully present: *Mannahatta, Paumanok*. Pre-European sounds can never become living words used in the present. They remain as traces, vestiges, and artifacts. If the sounds become words, the words can never become sentences; if the words become sentences, the sentences can never be spoken. There is no voice that can speak the past into the present, so as to create the impossible epic that would carry over the memory of a pre-European past into the contemporary moment of Whitman's New York. If he cannot fully bring the past into the present, neither can he, as a prophet would, fully bring into the present an image of the future.

Prophecy is an image of the future brought into the present. In Augustine's sense, it is the presence of future things. But prophetic poetry is no longer possible in the mid-nineteenth-century city. To experience an image of the future as a prophet would—namely, as vividly and overwhelmingly real—may have been the ultimate aim of Whitman, but the full possession of this prophetic power always remained an illusion. The images he saw of a post-European future—which is to say, a utopian and fully American future—were luminous vestiges that could never become real. Both the past and the future never became real enough; his poetry was neither epic enough, nor prophetic enough. Therein lies his uniqueness—an exemplarity that roots him in his historical and geographical moment. Whitman was engulfed in a present that refused to turn into either a future or a past.

Returning to Augustine's schema, everyone knows what memory is, and what it feels like. Everyone knows the nature of the longing expressed by Villon's *où sont les neiges d'antan,* "where are the snows of yesteryear." Everyone knows what it is for the past to be experienced again in the act of remembering. Everyone knows what hope is, and what expectation is—what it feels like to have an image of the future before the mind's eye. But what does it feel like to experience the present, or a "present image of a present thing"? More explicitly, and more prosaically, what could it mean that Augustine invokes an obscure verb, *contuere,* to name the act that seems so much more simple and more direct than the act of experiencing an image of either the past or the future? Our experience of the present is *contuitus.* We "see" (*tuere*), in some figural sense, the present. The term has been translated variously as "seeing," "direct perception," "direct sight," "immediate awareness," and so on.[17] But what is the figural sense of seeing, when we "see" a present image of the present? Memory and expectation, *memoria* and *expectatio,* are clear, both linguistically and in our own experience. But direct perception, or direct seeing, or simply the "seeing" of a present image in the present, is not clear, either linguistically, conceptually, or experientially. The meaning of the term *contuere,* which only appears in Augustine's time, is both seeing, in a sense that is not exactly literal, and "spiritual contemplation."[18]

Whitman and Baudelaire stare directly at the present. But their gaze is also a spiritual contemplation. Without the possibility of writing either epic, lyric, or prophetic poetry, they leave us with images of the present that refuse to turn into what poetry, traditionally, has always turned into. What remains is a simple gaze that transforms poetry into a spiritual contemplation—a desolate sense of looking, aware of its inability to either conjure the past or prophesy the future. The future is being prophesied as we speak, their poetry seems to say, by someone other than myself. Haussmann and his myriad future imitators are the new prophets; the city itself is the new prophet. There is no longer any need for poetry to bring an image of the past into the present because the past has lost its value. Neither is there any need for poetry to bring an image of the future into the present, because the present moment, now, is being transformed ceaselessly into an image of the future. It is being cut into as we speak, their poetry says, with paths through which the future can enter the city. The city is being imprinted with an ever more vivid picture of the future; and the city endlessly becomes this picture. The city is never there in the present; it is always about to become what it is. The present is already the abyss of the future. The vision of this process in the present is a spiritual contemplation—a vision of a gap inside of time in which the past has been cut off and the future is always about to arrive.

This is the dilemma that both Whitman and Baudelaire lead to. Their poetry, at the end of their lives, revolves around an increasingly empty time within time, a moment that is neither epic nor prophecy, neither memory nor expectation, when poetry can no longer allow itself to memorialize the past, and is no longer allowed to prophesy the future. In the mid-nineteenth century, cities are being created and re-created as images of future lives. The modern city as a present image of the lives that will be lived in it comes to replace a prophecy composed of words—namely, poetry. The avenues of Haussmann's city do not exist for the flaneur, but for the automobiles that do not yet exist, but are conjured by them. The city is an architectural prophecy that fulfills itself. Lives ever after will be lived in this way. There is no choice, no past to turn back to. Baudelaire gives in to despair at the thought that this is all that is left to poetry. The poet has become the minor acolyte of a city planner à la Haussmann, who explicitly says and enacts the fact that the past should not be memorialized, or ritually remembered, so much as effaced, cleared up, and made more hygienic. We must make room for the future: the city will be riddled with and transformed by the present image of future lives. In the same sense, Whitman is a witness to a time that has lost its balance. His New York, profoundly resistant to memorialization, and unable to remember its own past, becomes an empty site waiting for the advent of a future that never comes soon enough to fill the temporal void of the present. It is only by trying to understand this mid-nineteenth-century temporal hiatus—in which the past has lost its value, but the future has not yet arrived—that we can see how the afterlife of this anomalous temporality affects us still.

Notes

1. W. T. Bandy, "Whitman and Baudelaire," *Walt Whitman Quarterly Review* 1.3 (1983) 55.

2. Ibid., 53. This quotation from Baudelaire is in an essay entitled "Poetry of the Future," which appeared in the *North American Review* in February 1881. Whitman is arguing that American poets "labor under subordination of spirit, a lack of the concrete, and that modern aesthetic contagion . . . called the beauty disease."

3. James Woodress, ed., *Critical Essays on Walt Whitman* (Boston: G. K. Hall, 1983) 42. The review was published in the London *Critic* of April 1856.

4. See *Petits poèmes en prose,* ed. Robert Kopp (Paris: José Corti, 1968) lxiii. The review appeared in *Le Figaro,* February 7, 1864. In July 1857, the same critic from *Le Figaro* had published a vitriolic review of *Les Fleurs du mal,* in which he stigmatized the poems for their immorality. As a consequence, Baudelaire was sued by the government for offense to public and religious morals.

5. *The Nation and Atheneum,* December 18, 1926, 426.

6. See for instance David Weimer, *The City as Metaphor* (New York: Random House, 1966); K. Versluys, *The Poet in the City* (Tübingen: G. Narr Verlag, 1987) 52–55; and, for a more nuanced comparison, William C. Sharpe, *Unreal Cities* (Baltimore: Johns Hopkins UP, 1990) 72–75.

7. "Edgar Poe, sa vie, ses œuvres." In *Oeuvres complètes,* ed. Claude Pichois, 2 vols. (Paris: Gallimard/La Pléiade, 1975–76) 2:299. Subsequently referred to as *OC* followed by volume and page number.

8. "L'art philosophique," *OC,* 2:603. See Philippe Roger, *The American Enemy: A Story of French Anti-Americanism* (Chicago: U of Chicago P, 2005) 59–63.

9. Roger Asselineau, "When Walt Whitman Was a Parisian," *Mickle Street Review* 9.2 (1988) 30.

10. "France the 18th Year of these States." Walt Whitman, *Leaves of Grass and Other Writings,* ed. Michael Moon (New York: Norton, 2002) 198. All textual references to *Leaves of Grass* will be to this edition, an expanded and revised version of the 1973 Norton edition by Sculley Bradley and Harold W. Blodgett. Abbreviated as *LG* followed by page number.

11. Horace Traubel, *With Walt Whitman in Camden*, vol. 3 (1913; New York: Rowman and Littlefield, 1961) 35.

12. "Mon coeur mis à nu," *OC*, 1:686–87.

13. Walter Benjamin, "Zentralpark," in *Gesammelte Schriften*, ed. R. Tiedemann, vol. 1 (Frankfurt am Main: Suhrkamp, 1982) 682. Translation mine. In the immense set of notes known as *The Arcades Project*, Benjamin formulates the same thought word for word, but without the concluding question concerning Whitman (*Arcades*, J 66 a, 1). See Walter Benjamin, *Das Passagen-Werk*, ed. R. Tiedemann, 2 vols. (Frankfurt am Main: Suhrkamp, 1980); in English, *The Arcades Project*, trans. H. Eiland and K. McLaughlin (Cambridge: Cambridge UP, 1999).

14. Félix Nadar, *Charles Baudelaire intime* (1911; Neuchâtel: Ides et Calendes/La Bibliothèque des Arts, 1994) 36–37. Paraphrase mine. See also W. T. Bandy and Claude Pichois, *Baudelaire devant ses contemporains* (Monaco: Editions du Rocher, 1957) 15–34; and Benjamin, *The Arcades Project*, 248, 253, 259 (J11a, 2; J 14a, 2; J17, 6).

15. Including the Fulton Ferry Landing in Lower Manhattan.

16. "Préface des Fleurs," *OC*, 1:181.

17. See J. R. LeMaster and Donald D. Kummings, *Walt Whitman: An Encyclopedia* (New York: Garland, 1998) 232.

18. "L'oeuvre et la vie de Delacroix," *OC*, 2:751.

19. *Tout bon poète fut toujours* réaliste. "Puisque réalisme il y a," *OC*, 2:58.

20. See *LG*, 784.

21. Ezra Pound, *ABC of Reading* (New York: New Directions, 1960) 192.

22. "De l'héroïsme de la vie moderne." *OC*, 2:496.

23. See Jules Laforgue, *Mélanges posthumes* (Paris: Mercure de France, 1903) 113. On Laforgue and Whitman, see Betsy Erkkila, *Walt Whitman among the French: Poet and Myth* (Princeton: Princeton UP, 1980) 69–77. Had Laforgue published a complete translation of *Leaves of Grass*, he "would then have performed the same function for Whitman in France as Baudelaire had earlier performed for Edgar Poe" (Erkkila, 70).

24. Lucy Fountain, "Charles Pierre Baudelaire," *Lippincott's Magazine* 8 (October 1871) 384.

25. Eugene Benson, "Charles Baudelaire, Poet of the Malign," *Atlantic Monthly*, February 1869, 172. From an American point of view, Whitman was perceived as reacting against what Ann Douglas has termed "the feminization of American culture." *Leaves of Grass* was avowedly written for "a great composite Democratic Individual, male or female" (preface of 1872 edition), but many of the poems are addressed to a "Camerado" or "friend" who is self-evidently male. The sulfurous *Leaves of Grass* would not have been read by respectable women in Whitman's day, or at least not openly. See Ann Douglas, *The Feminization of American Culture* (New York: Avon P, 1977).

26. William James, "On a Certain Blindness in Human Beings," in *Talks to Teachers on Psychology and to Students on Some of Life's Ideals* (New York: Holt, 1899) 248; Walter Benjamin, "Paris, Capital of the Nineteenth Century," Exposé of 1939, *The Arcades Project*, 21.

27. Edwin G. Burrows and M. Wallace, *Gotham: A History of New York City to 1898* (Oxford: Oxford UP, 1999) 695.

28. Louis Veuillot, *Les Odeurs de Paris* (Paris, 1867; rpt. 1911) ix. Translation mine. Philip Hone is quoted in Burrows and Wallace, *Gotham*, 695.

29. "A Prankster," *OC*, 1:279.

30. *La France traverse une phase de vulgarité. Paris, centre et rayonnement de bêtise universelle.* "Projet de préface des *Fleurs du mal*," *OC*, 1:182.

31. "City of Ships," *LG*, 247.

32. Baudelaire, *Correspondance*, ed. Claude Pichois with Jean Ziegler (Paris: Gallimard, 1973) 1:599. Subsequently referred to as *Cor.*, followed by volume and page number.

CHAPTER 1

1. Louis Étienne, "Walt Whitman philosophe, poëte et 'rowdy,'" *La Revue européenne* (Paris), November 1861, 104–17. On Étienne's review, see Erkkila, *Whitman among the French*, 59–60. At the time, France was living under the authoritarian rule of Emperor Napoleon III. Erkkila emphasizes the political conservatism of Étienne, who was repelled by the democratic ideals embodied in Whitman's poetic persona.

2. Étienne, "Walt Whitman philosophe," 111.

3. See Clarence Godhes, "Whitman as 'One of the Roughs,'" *Walt Whitman Review* 8 (March 1962), rpt. in *Walt Whitman: Critical Assessments*, ed. William C. Sharpe, 4 vols. (Mountfield, East Sussex: Helm Information, 1995) 4:430–31.

4. Sharpe, *Walt Whitman: Critical Assessments*, 2:22.

5. Letter of September (?) 1866, Walt Whitman, *The Correspondence*, vols. 1–6, ed. Edwin Haviland Miller (New York: New York University P, 1961–77) 1:288.

6. Whitman, *Correspondence*, 1:348. The letter, written in October 1867, was to be transmitted to Moncure Conway, who was preparing an English edition of *Leaves of Grass*.

7. In Arthur Symons, *Charles Baudelaire: A Study* (London: E. Mathews, 1920), 11. On Swinburne's identification with Baudelaire, see Patricia Clements, "'Strange Flowers': Some Notes on the Baudelaire of Swinburne and Pater," *Modern Language Review* 76.1 (1981) 20–30.

8. A. C. Swinburne, "Charles Baudelaire," *The Complete Works of Algernon Charles Swinburne*, ed. Edmund Gosse and Thomas James Wise, vol. 13 (London: Heinemann, 1926) 418, 419.

9. A. C. Swinburne, "Whitmania," *Studies in Prose and Poetry* (London: Chatto and Windus, 1894) 140. On the complex relation between Swinburne and Whitman, see W. B. Cairns, "Swinburne's Opinion of Whitman," *American Literature* 3.2 (1931) 125–35; and Terry L. Meyers, "Swinburne and Whitman: Further Evidence," *Walt Whitman Quarterly Review* 14.1 (1996) 1–11.

10. Stendhal, *La chartreuse de Parme*, in *Œuvres complètes*, vol. 1 (Paris: Gallimard, 1952) 431. My translation. On Stendhal's hostility to America, see Roger, *The American Enemy*, 51–53.

11. Whitman's passion for the opera in New York has been extensively studied by Gay Wilson Allen, *The Solitary Singer: A Critical Biography of Walt Whitman* (Chicago: U of Chicago P, 1965) 112–15; Floyd Stovall, *The Foreground of "Leaves of Grass"* (Charlottesville: UP of Virginia, 1974) 79–100; and David Reynolds, *Walt Whitman's America: A Cultural Biography* (New York: Vintage, 1995) 154–93.

12. John T. Trowbridge, "Reminiscences of Walt Whitman," *Atlantic Monthly,* February 1902, 166.

13. As Edward K. Spann notes, the Astor Place Theater riot of 1849 was "a conflict of cultural as well as social style involving a popular urban culture whose animus counterpointed that of the elite." See *The New Metropolis: New York City, 1840–1857* (New York: Columbia UP, 1981) 235. In short, it was the Bowery taking up arms against Broadway. On May 10, 1849, a large mob gathered around the Astor Place, where Macready was playing Macbeth, and tried to force its way into the theater. In the ensuing confrontation with the policemen and militiamen who were protecting the building, twenty-two people died, "including an old man waiting for a horsecar on the Bowery and an eight-year old boy" (Spann, 238).

14. See Gene Lalor, "Whitman among the New York Literary Bohemians: 1859–62," *Walt Whitman Review* 25.4 (1979) 131–45.

15. Christine Stansell, "Whitman at Pfaff's: Commercial Culture, Literary Life and New York Bohemia at Mid-Century," *Walt Whitman Quarterly Review* 10.3 (1993) 110.

16. Lewis Mumford, *The City in History: Its Origins, Its Transformations and Its Prospects* (New York: Harcourt Brace, 1961) 422.

17. See Spann, *The New Metropolis,* 23–44; F. Weil, *A History of New York,* trans. J. Gladding (New York: Columbia UP, 2004); and R. Burns and J. Sanders, *New York: An Illustrated History* (New York: Knopf, 1999) 68–125.

18. *The Uncollected Poetry and Prose of Walt Whitman,* ed. Emory Holloway (Gloucester, Mass.: Peter Smith, 1972) 93. The article was published in the *American Review* in November 1845.

19. Ibid., 92.

20. See Burrows and Wallace, *Gotham,* 736.

21. See M. Wynn Thomas, "Whitman's Tale of Two Cities," *American Literary History* 6.4 (1994) 635.

22. "Our City," *Walt Whitman of the New York Aurora,* ed. Charles H. Brown and Joseph Jay Rubin (Carrolltown, Pa.: Bald Eagle P, 1950) 17.

23. Charles Dickens, *American Notes and Pictures from Italy* (New York: Macmillan, 1903; rpt. London: Chapman & Hall, 1842) 74–75.

24. Jerome Loving, *Walt Whitman: The Song of Himself* (Berkeley: U of California P, 1999) 59. Whitman alludes to the cane in the piece entitled "A Lazy Day" (Brown and Rubin, *Whitman of the Aurora,* 44).

25. Charles Baudelaire, "The Painter of Modern Life," in *Selected Writings on Art and Artists,* ed. and trans. P. E. Charvet (Cambridge: Cambridge UP, 1972) 421.

26. Ibid., 420.

27. Thomas L. Brasher, *Whitman as Editor of the "Brooklyn Daily Eagle"* (Detroit: Wayne State UP, 1970) 37–84.

28. Loving, *The Song of Himself,* 103.

29. *Whitman in his own Time,* ed. Joel Myerson (Iowa city: U of Iowa Press, 1991) 43.

30. Quoted by Thomas, "Whitman's Tale of Two Cities," 632.

31. "At One O'Clock in the Morning," *OC,* 1:287.

32. "Mannahatta," *LG,* 397.

33. "Song of Myself," sec. 42, ll. 1075–77, *LG,* 67.

34. *Notes and Fragments Left by Walt Whitman and Now Edited by Dr. Richard Maurice Bucke, His Literary Executor* (Ontario: A. Talbot, 1899), part 3, n. 126. In Whitman's time, "New York" meant "Manhattan."

35. Peter Conrad, "The Epic City," *The Art of the City: Views and Versions of New York* (Oxford: Oxford UP, 1984) 8.

36. Alan Trachtenberg, "Whitman's Lesson of the City," in *Breaking Bounds: Whitman and American Cultural Studies,* ed. Betsy Erkkila and Jay Grossman (Oxford: Oxford UP, 1996) 164.

37. M. Wynn Thomas, "Walt Whitman and Mannahatta–New York," *American Quarterly* 34.4 (1982) 364.

38. "Give Me the Splendid Silent Sun."

39. Brown and Rubin, *Whitman of the Aurora,* 26, 54.

40. *LG,* 591.

41. Charles Baudelaire, *The Flowers of Evil,* trans. Keith Waldrop (Middletown, Conn.: Wesleyan UP, 2006) 123. I have selected this translation not only because of Waldrop's uncanny ability to capture the radical modernity of Baudelaire's voice, but also because its proselike cadences echo Whitman's unrhymed verse.

42. Ibid.

43. "Two City Areas, Certain Hours," *Specimen Days and Collect* (1883; New York: Dover, 1995) 134.

44. M. Wynn Thomas has argued that Whitman uses this "holistic descriptive language of riverine flow, of oceanic tides, or of electric currents" as "totalizing images that resist the very idea of subdivision and create the illusion of a single, unsegregated urban scene" ("Whitman's Tale of Two Cities," 648). I am envisaging these images from the opposite direction—not as tokens of democratic inclusion but as signs of the poet's effacement from his own poems in the face of the oceanic city.

45. Conrad, *Art of the City,* 17. See also Thomas, "Mannahatta–New York," 365.

46. Baudelaire, *Flowers of Evil,* 116.

47. "Song of Myself," sec. 26, l. 586, *LG,* 49.

48. "Song of Myself," sec. 8, ll. 154–57, *LG,* 32.

49. Whitman, *Notes and Fragments,* 40.

50. Horace Traubel, *With Walt Whitman in Camden,* vol. 2 (1907; rpt. New York: Rowman and Littlefield, 1961) 246.

51. Whitman, *Specimen Days and Collect,* 18. "(I suppose the critics will laugh heartily, but the influence of these Broadway omnibus jaunts and drivers, and declamations and escapades undoubtedly enter'd into the gestation of *Leaves of Grass*)," Whitman adds (19).

52. "Song of Myself," sec. 42, l. 1078, *LG*, 67.

53. "Song of Myself," sec. 16, ll. 330–34, *LG*, 39. This passage already appeared as such in the first edition of *Leaves of Grass*.

54. "Song of Myself" is Whitman's longest, most ambitious, and perhaps most puzzling poem. As Roy Harvey Pearce phrased it in 1961, "Most students of 'Song of Myself' have wished to find in it some firm structural principle." According to Malcolm Cowley, the poem was misread as a catalog of popular American culture, whereas its true inspiration would be found in Eastern philosophy. Roy Harvey Pearce has argued that "Song of Myself" represents "the clearest, surest . . . and most widely gauged product of Whitman's desire to create an American epic." Raymond Cook has emphasized Whitman's identification with external objects; and Graham Clarke has categorized "Song of Myself" as a theatrical performance, emphasizing the power of the voice. All these important essays are in Sharpe, *Walt Whitman: Critical Assessments*, 2:234–343.

55. Edgar Allan Poe, "The Man of the Crowd," in *Poetry and Tales*, ed. Patrick McQuinn (New York: Library of America, 1984) 388, 389.

56. See Baudelaire, "Painter of Modern Life," 397.

57. "Crossing Brooklyn Ferry," *LG*, 162–63, l .70, ll. 74–75.

58. In a letter of February 6, 1853, Baudelaire is looking for a journal to publish his translation of Poe's "The Man of the Crowd." Baudelaire's translation finally appeared in *Le Pays* in January 1855 under the title "L'homme des foules." See Raymond Poggenburg, *Charles Baudelaire: Une micro-histoire* (Paris: Corti, 1987) 134, 163.

59. See Edgar Allan Poe, *Doings of Gotham*, ed. T. Olive Mabbott (Pottsville, Pa.: Jacob E. Spannuth, 1929).

60. James, "On a Certain Blindness," 250.

61. Loving, *The Song of Himself*, 219.

62. See M. Wynn Thomas, *The Lunar Light of Whitman's Poetry* (Cambridge: Harvard UP, 1987) 92–116. Another illuminating contribution to the lively debate on "Crossing Brooklyn Ferry" is Roger Gilbert, "From Anxiety to Power: Grammar and Crisis in 'Crossing Brooklyn Ferry,'" *Nineteenth Century Literature* 42.3 (1987) 339–61. Gilbert proposes an optimistic reading of "Crossing Brooklyn Ferry," but one that breaks away from the traditional Emersonian readings. Gilbert argues that Whitman's victorious struggle with death is figured as "a struggle to cross *out* of writing and into speech, into a form of language associated with life and power, not death and absence" (341).

63. "Crossing Brooklyn Ferry," stanzas 1 and 2.

64. Sec. 3, l. 23, *LG*, 136. Emphasis mine.

65. *Leaves of Grass, Facsimile of the 1860 Edition*, ed. Roy Harvey Pearce (Ithaca: Cornell UP, 1961) 384.

66. Dana Brand, "Immense Phantom Concourse: Whitman and the Urban Crowds," *The Spectator and the City in Nineteenth Century American Literature* (Cambridge: Cambridge UP, 1991) 168–69.

67. Sec. 2, ll. 6–7, *LG*, 135–36.

68. Sec. 3, l. 33. The disappearance of the poet's body could also be seen as an apotheosis, since his head is now crowned with an aureole. For an analysis of Whitman's dark view of the city and a comparison with Poe, see Graham Clarke,

Walt Whitman: The Poem as Private History (New York: St Martin's, 1991), esp. chap. 5, "'The Sleepers': Whitman's City of Dreadful Night," 99–126.

69. See Maria Farland, "Decomposing City: Walt Whitman's New York and the Science of Life and Death," *ELH* 74 (2007) 799–827.

70. Quoted by ibid., 807.

71. "This Compost," ll. 6, 9, *LG,* 368.

72. Whitman, *Notes and Fragments,* part 1, 9 n. 1. This draft is antecedent to the 1855 edition. Fragments from this draft were used by Whitman in the second stanza of "The Sleepers" ("A shroud I see and I am a shroud").

73. "Crossing Brooklyn Ferry," sec. 2, l. 9, *LG,* 136.

74. "Song of Myself," sec. 42, l. 1054.

75. Trachtenberg, "Whitman's Lesson of the City," 169.

76. "Do I contradict myself? / Very well then I contradict myself / (I am large, I contain multitudes)." "Song of Myself," sec. 51, ll. 1324–26, *LG,* 88.

77. "There Was a Child Went Forth," ll. 30–31, *LG,* 307.

78. Whitman, *Notes and Fragments,* part 1, 40 n. 133.

79. Ibid., 44 n. 147.

80. Thomas, "Whitman's Tale of Two Cities," 654. See also Ed Cutler, "Passage to Modernity: *Leaves of Grass* and the 1853 Crystal Palace Exhibition in New York," *Walt Whitman Quarterly Review* 16.2 (1998) 65–89.

81. "A Visit to Plumbe's Gallery," *The Gathering of the Forces,* ed. Cleveland Rogers and John Black, vol. 2 (New York: Putnam's, 1920) 116. On the striking similarities between "A Visit to Plumbe's Gallery" and "Crossing Brooklyn Ferry," see Brand, "Immense Phantom Concourse," 163–70.

82. See Keith F. Davis, *The Origins of American Photography 1839–1885* (New Haven: Yale UP, 2008) 24–25.

83. Edmond de Goncourt and Jules de Goncourt, *Journal: Mémoires de la vie littéraire,* vol. 1 (Paris: R. Laffont, 1989) 224. My translation. See Philippe Hamon, *Imageries: Littérature et image au XIXe siècle* (Paris: J. Corti, 2001) 73.

84. Charles Baudelaire, "Le public moderne et la photographie," *OC,* 2:614–19.

CHAPTER 2

1. P[hineas] T[aylor] Barnum, *Struggles and Triumphs,* ed. Carl Bode (Harmondsworth: Penguin, 1981) 102, 103. The Penguin text is based on the expanded second edition of the memoirs, published in 1869.

2. Ibid.

3. Brasher, *Whitman as Editor,* 41–42. See also Loving, *The Song of Himself,* 165. The anecdote may be apocryphal, but there can be no doubt that Whitman was familiar with P. T. Barnum.

4. On Whitman as a "freak," see Reynolds, *Walt Whitman's America,* 304–6.

5. Adrienne Siegel, *The Image of the City in Popular Literature 1820–1870* (Port Washington, N.Y.: Kennikat P, 1981) 136, 137.

6. Luc Sante, *Low Life: Lures and Snares of Old New York,* rev. ed. (New York: Farrar, Straus and Giroux, 2003) 355.

7. *LG,* 107.

8. *Oxford English Dictionary.*

9. For a detailed account of tableaux vivants in nineteenth-century New York, see Jack McCullough, *Living Pictures on the New York Stage* (Ann Arbor: UMI Research P, 1983).

10. In all of these novels, set in an upper-class background, the tableau vivant coincides with a moment of extreme dramatic intensity, and allegorizes the particular predicament of a character. For an illustrated study of photographed tableaux vivants in nineteenth-century England, including the works of Lewis Carroll, see *Tableaux vivants: Fantaisies photographiques victoriennes, 1840–1880* (Paris: Édition de la Réunion des Musées Nationaux, 1999).

11. Barry Faulk, *Music-Hall and Modernity: The Late-Victorian Discovery of Popular Culture* (Athens: Ohio UP, 2004) 150. The club in question was the Suffolk Home club in Leicester Square. The quotation is by the journalist George Augustus Sala.

12. See M. Christine Boyer, *The City of Collective Memory: Its Historical Imagery and Architectural Entertainments* (Cambridge: MIT P, 1994). Boyer shows that the city and the theater have long been intertwined as "ordering experiences" of the chaos of everyday life (74). Until the end of the nineteenth century, she argues, "the city as a work of art carried a sense of moral order within its aesthetic forms" (74).

13. Sante, *Low Life*, 355.

14. Whitman, *Correspondence*, 2:57.

15. See Eric de Kuyper and Emile Poppe, "Voir et regarder," *Communications* 34 (1981) 86.

16. Conrad, "The Epic City," 18.

17. "From Montauk Point," an 1888 poem from "Sands at Seventy," *LG*, 426.

18. Sec. 9, l. 104, *LG*, 139.

19. *LG*, 397. See Thomas, "Whitman's Tale of Two Cities," 636.

20. Conrad, "The Epic City," 18. For an analysis of panoramic views in *Leaves of Grass* and, more generally, of Whitman's visual perception of New York, see James Dougherty, *Walt Whitman and the Citizen's Eye* (Baton Rouge: Louisiana State UP, 1993) 139–71. On the influence of panoramas on Whitman's poetics, see also Charles Zarobila, "Walt Whitman and the Panorama," *Walt Whitman Review* 25.1 (1979) 51–59.

21. Jonathan Crary, *Techniques of the Observer: On Vision and Modernity in the Nineteenth Century* (Cambridge: MIT P, 1992) 20.

22. Edmund Burke, *A Philosophical Enquiry into the Origins of our Ideas of the Sublime and the Beautiful* (1757; Oxford: Oxford UP, 1990) 67.

23. "Out of the Rolling Ocean the Crowd," *LG*, 92.

24. *LG*, 438. The poem was composed in 1888 by a sixty-nine-year-old Whitman.

25. *Specimen Days and Collect*, 117, 118. In an earlier section entitled "My Passion for Ferries," Whitman writes: "What oceanic currents, eddies underneath— the great tides of humanity also, with ever-shifting movements" (17).

26. See Antoine Compagnon, *Baudelaire devant l'innombrable* (Paris: Presses de l'Université Sorbonne-Nouvelle, 2003) 101–33.

27. *Flowers of Evil*, 117–18.

28. William Shakespeare, *The Tempest,* IV.i, *The Riverside Shakespeare,* ed. Harry Levin et al. (Boston: Houghton Mifflin, 1974) 1631.

29. Michel Foucault, *Discipline and Punish: The Birth of the Prison,* trans. Alan Sheridan (New York: Pantheon, 1979) 217.

30. See Crary, *Techniques of the Observer,* and Jonathan Crary, "Spectacle, Attention, Counter-Memory," *October* 50 (1989) 96–107, esp. 105.

31. For a detailed account of the embassy, see Masao Miyoshi, *As We Saw Them: The First Japanese Embassy to the United States* (Berkeley: U of California P, 1979). Miyoshi dismisses the poem as "one of Whitman's usual longwinded catalogues" (30). I naturally take issue with such a description.

32. *LG,* 203–4.

33. In "A Song of the Rolling Earth," Whitman praises "him who makes the dictionaries of words that print cannot touch" (*LG,* 188). See Henri Meschonnic, *Les états de la poétique* (Paris: PUF, 1985), and *Critique du rythme: Anthropologie historique du langage* (La Grasse: Verdier, 1982).

34. In a newspaper article, Whitman pointed out that the crowded deck of a ferryboat offered him "a swift view of the phantom-like semblance of humanity, as it is sometimes seen in dreams." See "Philosophy of Ferries," August 13, 1847, in Rogers and Black, *Gathering of the Forces,* 159–66. See also "My Passion for Ferries," *Specimen Days and Collect,* 16–17.

35. *Flowers of Evil,* 133.

36. *LG,* 263.

37. "To a Stranger," *LG,* 109.

38. Walter Benjamin, *Charles Baudelaire: A Lyric Poet in the High Era of Capitalism,* trans. Harry Zohn (London: Verso, 1983) 45.

39. See Betsy Erkkila, "Whitman and the Homosexual Republic," in *Walt Whitman: The Centennial Essays,* ed. Ed Folsom (Iowa City: U of Iowa P, 1994) 153–71. Erkkila argues that Whitman creates "an amalgam between loving men and democracy," which, "in its most visionary realization . . . will give rise to a city—and ultimately an American republic—in which loving men can live and love and touch openly" (158–59). Another important contribution is Thomas Yingling, "Homosexuality and Utopian Discourse in American Poetry," in Erkkila and Grossman, *Breaking Bounds,* 135–46. For Yingling, Whitman envisions a utopian homosexual community in "Calamus," and "grounds [his] poetry in a homocentric vision of unity and transcendent possibility against which [he] test[ed] an imperfect 'America'" (139). In *Disseminating Whitman* (Cambridge: Harvard UP, 1991), Michael Moon argues that Whitman pictures homosexual relations as being more "fluid" than heterosexual ones, and, hence, of greater importance in achieving the poetic and social dissemination he is aiming at. See also Robert K. Martin, *The Homosexual Tradition in American Poetry* (Austin: U of Texas P, 1979), and M. Jimmie Killingsworth, *Whitman's Poetry of the Body: Sexuality, Politics and the Text* (Chapel Hill: U of North Carolina P, 1979).

40. "Sparkles from the Wheel," *LG,* 328.

41. " Song of Myself," sec. 42, ll. 1075–82, *LG,* 77.

42. *LG,* 263.

43. Whitman, *Democratic Vistas,* in *Specimen Days and Collect,* 212.

44. See Reynolds, *Walt Whitman's America,* 108–10; and Thomas, "Mannahatta–New York."

45. "Mannahatta," *LG,* 397.

46. Quoted in Reynolds, *Walt Whitman's America,* 108.

47. In another poem from "Drum-Taps," "City of Ships," also written in 1865, toward the close of the Civil War, New York is envisioned from a political and military perspective, as a city at war: "Spring up O City—not for peace alone, but be indeed yourself, warlike!" *LG,* 246.

48. See Whitman, *Specimen Days and Collect,* 29–81.

49. Whitman, *Democratic Vistas,* 209.

50. Sec. 2, ll. 21–25, *LG,* 204.

51. For another view on history as a cyclical process, culminating in a circular journey around the earth, see "Passage to India" (1871). *LG,* 345–53.

52. In the wake of Walter Benjamin, much has been written about Baudelaire's response to the violence of modernity and the trauma of history. Ross Chambers, for one, has analyzed "To A Woman Passing By" not as a love poem, but as a poem about "history as a devastating *passing-by* that gets our attention only to leave us stunned and devastated." In Baudelaire's "*écriture du désastre,*" Chambers argues, pointing ahead to Maurice Blanchot, history is "that factor of noise and disturbance, of *étourdissement.*" See Ross Chambers, "Heightening the Lowly: Baudelaire's 'Je n'ai pas oublié . . .' and 'À une passante,'" *Nineteenth Century French Studies* 33.1–2 (2008) 48, 49.

53. "Song of Myself," sec. 15, ll. 273, 304–6, *LG,* 37–38. For an enlightening parallelism, see Graham Clarke's reading of "The Sleepers" as "the quintessential poem of New York" in which the city is "imagined as a series of dark, frightening and disparate experiences . . . emblematic of institutions that Whitman railed against: asylums, prisons and hospitals" (*Poem as Private History,* 109).

54. Baudelaire, *Artificial Edens, OC,* 1:392.

55. This is a collage of quotations all taken from section 8 of "Song of Myself" (*LG,* 32).

56. See Simon Parker, "Unrhymed Modernity: New York City, the Popular Newspaper Page, and the Forms of Whitman's Poetry," *Walt Whitman Quarterly Review* 16.3–4 (1999) 161–71.

57. Baudelaire, *OC,* 2:822. There are many critical allusions to newspapers in Baudelaire's intimate journals and in his notebooks on Belgium.

58. Sec. 2, l. 33, *LG,* 204.

CHAPTER 3

1. This point was not lost on Haussmann's numerous enemies. In an essay published twelve years after the *grands travaux* had begun, Victor Fournel claimed that Haussmann's boulevards were not designed to embellish the capital, but to facilitate the circulation of soldiers through Paris and to ward off potential revolutions. See *Paris nouveau et Paris futur* (Paris: J. Lecoffre, 1865) 29–37.

2. See L. Réau et al., *L'oeuvre du baron Haussmann, Préfet de la Seine* (Paris: PUF, 1954) 35–36. *C'était l'éventrement du vieux Paris, du quartier des émeutes, des*

barricades par une large voie centrale perçant de part en part ce dédale impraticable (Baron Haussmann, *Mémoires*, 3:54, quoted by Réau et al., 60).

3. See David H. Pinkney, *Napoleon III and the Rebuilding of Paris* (Princeton: Princeton UP, 1968) 91–92.

4. *Je n'ai jamais arrêté le tracé d'une voie quelconque, et à plus forte raison celui d'une artère principale, sans me préoccuper du point de vue qu'on pouvait lui donner.* Haussmann, *Mémoires*, 3:530, quoted in Réau et al., *L'oeuvre du baron Haussmann*, 71.

5. As Shelley Rice notes in her fascinating study of early photographs of Paris, "The attachment to the narrow passages and crumbling stones of the Old Paris was not shared by most people living there in the 1830s and 1840s. . . . Most Parisians during these years perceived [these streets] as dirty, crowded and un-healthy. Covered with mud and makeshift shanties, damp and fetid, filled with the signs of poverty as well as . . . garbage and waste . . . these narrow roads hardly seemed worth celebrating." S. Rice, *Parisian Views* (Cambridge: MIT P, 1987) 8–9.

6. In 1860, eleven previously independent communes adjoining Paris were incorporated into the city by Haussmann so as to form a *grand Paris*, twice as large in surface area, with a total population of over one and a half million. Before 1860, Paris included twelve arrondissements: after 1860, the number jumped to twenty, and the population rose to 1,696,000 people. See Bernard Marchand, *Paris: Histoire d'une ville* (Paris: Seuil/Histoire, 1993) 91; and D. H. Pinkney, *Rebuilding of Paris*, 151–73.

7. Maxime Du Camp, *Paris, ses organes, ses fonctions, sa vie dans la seconde moitié du XIXe siècle* (6 vols, 1883), 6:253. A modern defender of Haussmann would point out that in addition to creating the new boulevards, the *Préfet de la Seine* also vastly improved the hygiene in the city by redesigning the sewer system and facilitating the access to clean water.

8. About Haussmann's radical redesigning of the Île de la Cité, see Réau et al., *L'oeuvre du baron Haussmann*, 53–54; and Pinkney, *Rebuilding of Paris*, 87–90.

9. In 1847, Paris had 8,600 gaslit streetlamps; in 1866, more than 30,000. Haussmann also improved the lighting inside the buildings. See Pinkney, *Rebuilding of Paris*, 72–73.

10. "L'Exposition universelle de 1855," *OC*, 2:580.

11. See *Cor.*, 2:197, letter dated December 20, 1861, to Arsène Houssaye: *Je crois que j'ai enfin trouvé un titre qui rend bien mon idée:* LA LUEUR ET LA FUMÉE, POÈMES EN PROSE.

12. *Poèmes nocturnes (essais de poésie lyrique en prose, dans le genre de Gaspard de la Nuit).* Letter to Armand du Mesnil, February 9, 1861, *Cor.* 2:128.

13. *Cor.*, 2:254.

14. Benjamin, *The Arcades Project*, 336.

15. *Hôpital, lupanar, purgatoire, enfer, bagne. . . . Je t'aime, ô capitale infâme!* "Projet d'épilogue pour l'édition de 1861," *OC*, 1:191. *O cité ! . . . éprise du plaisir jusqu'à l'atrocité*, "Les Aveugles," *OC*, 1:92.

16. *Je rentre dans l'enfer (Paris)*, letter from 1860, *Cor.* 2:101; *Paris m'est mauvais*, letter to his mother, 1861, *Cor.* 2:154; *Tu ne saurais croire jusqu'à quel point la race parisienne est dégradée*, letter to his mother, 1862, *Cor.* 2:254.

17. *The Prose Poems and La Fanfarlo,* trans. Rosemary Lloyd (New York: Oxford UP, 1991) 30. The translation will be abbreviated as *PP,* followed by page number. I have frequently modified the translation or relied on my own.

18. In the "Parisian Scenes," Baudelaire speaks of "the cities" or "the old capitals" (*Quand, ainsi qu'un poète, il descend dans les villes* . . . ; *Dans les plis sinueux des vieilles capitales.* . . .). There are no details that would positively identify Paris as Paris, except in "The Swan," where the Place du Carrousel is mentioned by name.

19. See "To A Passerby" and "The Sun" ("Parisian Scenes"); in the *Petits poèmes en prose,* "Miss Scalpel," "The Eyes of the Poor," etc.

20. The poem entitled "The Rag-Pickers' Wine" begins in the heart of an old faubourg, "muddy labyrinth / Where people swarm and storms brew" (*Au coeur d'un vieux faubourg, labyrinthe fangeux / Où l'humanité grouille en ferments orageux*).

21. See Eric Hazan, *L'invention de Paris* (Paris: Seuil, 2002) 419–21.

22. See W. Benjamin: "A criterion for deciding whether or not the city is modern: the absence of monuments. 'New York is a city without monuments' (Döblin)" (*The Arcades Project,* 385). On the questionable, but widespread, belief that "the United States have no monuments," see D. Rouillard, "L'Amérique n'a pas de monuments," in *Américanisme et modernité: l'idéal américain dans l'architecture,* ed. J.-L. Cohen and H. Damisch (Paris: Presses de l'EHESS/Flammarion, 1993) 51–74.

23. Walter Benjamin, "On Some Motifs in Baudelaire," in *Illuminations,* trans. Harry Zohn, ed. Hannah Arendt (New York: Schocken, 1969) 138.

24. Goncourt and Goncourt, *Journal,* 632. See T. J. Clark, *The Painting of Modern Life: Paris in the Art of Manet and His Followers,* rev. ed. (Princeton: Princeton UP, 1999) 35.

25. Clark, *Painting of Modern Life,* 35.

26. "Edgar Poe, sa vie, ses œuvres, " *OC,* 2:297.

27. Ibid., 2:299.

28. *Il vous suffirait d'une journée dans notre triste, dans notre ennuyeux Paris, dans notre Paris-New York, pour vous guérir radicalement. Cor.,* 1:599.

29. *Un port noir et américain.* Letter to Narcisse Ancelle, *Cor.,* 2:408.

30. "Recueillement," *OC,* 1:140.

31. I am generalizing from the "Spleen et Idéal" section of *Les Fleurs du Mal,* which contains Baudelaire's most intimate confessions.

32. See Compagnon, *Baudelaire devant l'innombrable,* 115–33. As Compagnon points out, "The street is both the site of the poem and its model, its *topos*" (131).

33. *J'aime passionnément le mystère, parce que j'ai toujours l'espoir de le débrouiller. Je me laissai donc entraîner par cette compagne, ou plutôt par cette énigme inespérée.* Poem XLVII. *OC,* 1:353. *PP,* 99. Translation modified.

34. *Fusées. OC,* 1:649. My translation.

35. *OC,* 1:651. My translation.

36. *Pour le parfait flâneur, pour l'observateur passionné, c'est une immense jouissance d'élire domicile dans le nombre, dans l'ondoyant, dans le fugitif et l'infini.* "Le peintre de la vie moderne," *OC,* 2:691. My translation.

37. See *Petits poèmes en prose,* 281. In Baudelaire's own words, "The beautiful Dorothea" is a "souvenir de l'Ile Bourbon," an island now known as Mauritius.

"Mademoiselle Bistouri"—usually translated into English as "Miss Scalpel"—is a nickname, either coined by the woman's consorts or of Baudelaire's invention. Prostitutes almost universally adopted a nom de guerre in nineteenth-century Paris. As documented in Alexandre Parent-Duchâtelet's magisterial study *De la prostitution dans la ville de Paris* (1836), low-ranking prostitutes were often given grotesque pseudonyms inspired by their physical characteristics—e.g., "Lou-chon" (cross-eye), "Boule-de-Suif" (Butterball)—or by their personalities. "Miss Scalpel" appears to be Baudelaire's ironic twist on the prostitute's nom de guerre.

38. See *Petits poèmes en prose*, 303. The boy, whose name is unknown, also posed for some of Manet's paintings. Several contemporary testimonies attest to the authenticity of the story. The horrifying notion of recuperating the rope for its properties of "luck" is a common folklore motif (see for example Nerval's 1832 story "La Main de Gloire").

39. Regarding the identity of the "mistress" in the poem, see *Petits poèmes en prose*, 339. See also the ink sketches of Berthe by Baudelaire in *Baudelaire: Documents iconographiques*, ed. Claude Pichois and François Ruchon (Geneva: Pierre Cailler, 1960) plates 142, 143, 144.

40. *Le poète, l'artiste:* in "The Crowds" and in "The *Confiteor* of the Artist," *PP*, 85.

41. *OC*, 2:692.

42. *Un promeneur solitaire et pensif. . . . Il entre, comme il le veut, dans le personnage de chacun . . . adopte comme siennes toutes les professions, toutes les joies et toutes les misères que la circonstance lui présente.* Poem XII, *OC*, 1:291; *PP*, 44.

43. An obvious reminiscence of Jean-Jacques Rousseau's *Rêveries d'un promeneur solitaire.*

44. *PP*, 44.

45. *Je désire surtout que mon maudit gazetier me laisse m'amuser à ma guise. 'Vous n'éprouvez donc jamais, me dit-il . . . le besoin de partager vos jouissances?' Voyez-vous le subtil envieux! Il sait que je dédaigne les siennes, et il vient s'insinuer dans les miennes. . . . OC*, 1:313. My translation.

46. *Je n'aime rien tant qu'être seul.* Letter from Brussels to Madame Aupick, March 5, 1866 (*Cor.*, 2:625). Baudelaire was concerned that his poetry was attracting more and more attention among the younger generation of poets in Paris; Verlaine had recently published an enthusiastic essay on *Les Fleurs du mal* in the literary review *L'Art.* As Baudelaire admitted to his mother, the last thing he wanted was the creation of a "Baudelairian" school of poetry.

47. "The Gallant Marksman," "The Eyes of the Poor," "The Soup and the Clouds" are addressed to Baudelaire's mistress; "The Dog and the Flask" to a dog; "The Good Dogs" to the dogs of Paris.

48. "The Wild Woman and the Sweetheart," "Let Us Beat Up the Poor," "The Bad Glazier."

49. Baudelaire (or his stand-in) is the main protagonist in "The Bad Glazier" and "At One O' Clock in the Morning." He speaks as a witness or spectator in poems such as "The Prankster" and "The Poor Child's Toy." He is invisible in "The Old Woman's Despair" and "The Rope."

50. January 15, 1866, from Brussels, *Cor.* 2:583. *Joseph Delorme* is the title of a

book by Sainte-Beuve that loosely mixes poetic passages with philosophical musings.

51. Walter Benjamin, "The Storyteller," *Illuminations*, 83–84.

52. *Il se pourrait bien que je renonçasse à publier la suite des Poèmes en prose, qui faisaient quinze feuilletons.* Letter to Madame Aupick, September 22, 1862 (*Cor.*, 2:261).

53. See *Petits poèmes en prose*, ix. The written note in Baudelaire's handwriting is in the Bibliothèque littéraire Jacques Doucet in Paris.

54. In 1857, the poems that are now poems XXIV ("Plans"), XXVI ("The Eyes of the Poor"), XXVII ("A Hero's Death"), and XXVIII ("The Counterfeit Coin") appeared in *Le Présent*, under the title *Poèmes nocturnes*. The first poems to appear in print were poem XXII ("Evening Twilight") and poem XXIII ("Solitude"), which were published in *L'hommage à C. F. Denecourt* in 1855.

55. See letter to the publisher Jules Hetzel, October 8, 1963: *Dans le* Spleen de Paris *il y aura cent morceaux—il en manque encore trente* (*Cor.*, 2:324).

56. See *Cor.*, 2:283 (*POEMES EN PROSE, Presque faits*), 301 (*Le* Spleen de Paris *est inachevé, et n'a pas été livré à temps. Il ne faut, pour le finir, qu'une quinzaine de jours de travail, mais de travail vigoureux*), 305 (*Je viens de recevoir des épreuves du* Spleen de Paris, *mon Dieu! que ce sera long à finir!*), 395 (*Je me figure que je ne saurai jamais achever ce livre interrompu depuis si longtemps*), etc.

57. *Et pour comble de ridicule il FAUT qu'au milieu de ces insupportables secousses qui m'usent je fasse des vers.* Cor., 1:311.

58. Baudelaire, *Cor*, 1:327. Letter dated December 20, 1855.

59. Letter to his mother, March 3, 1864: *Je suis tombé dans une hideuse léthargie.* Cor., 2:350.

60. *Le seul éloge que je sollicite pour ce livre, est qu'on reconnaisse qu'il n'est pas un pur album, et qu'il a un commencement et une fin.* Cor. 2:196.

61. *Enlevez une vertèbre, et les deux morceaux de cette tortueuse fantaisie se rejoindront sans peine. Hachez-la en de nombreux fragments, et vous verrez que chacun peut exister à part.* OC, 1:275; *PP*, 30. The metaphor of the serpent is to be found in the "Reliquat," which contains Baudelaire's notes toward the dedication: *Enfin, petits tronçons. Tout le serpent.* OC, 1:366.

62. *OC*, 1:275; *PP*, 30.

63. *Un oeil expérimenté ne s'y trompe jamais. Dans ces traits rigides ou abattus, dans ces yeux caves et ternes, ou brillants des derniers éclairs de la lutte, dans ces rides profondes et nombreuses, dans ces démarches lentes et si saccadées, il déchiffre tout de suite les innombrables légendes de l'amour trompé, du dévouement inconnu, des efforts non récompensés, de la faim et du froid humblement, silencieusement supportés.* OC, 1:292; *PP*, 45. Translation modified.

64. See for example Cicero, *De inventione* II.2.1–3. Ancient passages on Zeuxis, Helen, and the models for Helen are collected in A. Reinach, *Textes grecs et latins relatifs à l'histoire de la peinture ancienne* (Paris: C. Klincksieck, 1921) 194–98.

65. George Poulet, *Exploding Poetry: Baudelaire/Rimbaud*, trans. Françoise Meltzer (Chicago: U of Chicago P, 1984) 61.

66. Poem XXXV, *OC*, 1:339.

67. *OC*, 1:662. My translation. The word *poncif*, already in usage in the six-

teenth century, originally meant "stencil." It came to signify "conventional drawing," and then, figuratively, a cliché, or commonplace. On Baudelaire and the *poncif,* see Benjamin, *The Arcades Project,* 322, 333, 335. For an analysis of *poncif* and its English equivalent (cliché) in Baudelaire and Benjamin, see Elissa Marder, *Dead Time: Temporal Disorders in the Wake of Modernity* (Stanford: Stanford UP, 2001) 78–87.

68. *OC,* 1:670.

69. "Salon de 1846," *OC,* 2:468. "Le Voyage." English translation by Roy Campbell in *Poems of Baudelaire: A Translation of "Les Fleurs du Mal"* (New York: Pantheon, 1962) 176.

70. On the *lieu commun* as a substitute for an experience of the world that has become impossible, see Giorgio Agamben, *Infancy and History: Essays on the Destruction of Experience,* trans. Liz Heron (London: Verso, 1993) 42. For Agamben, Baudelaire's search for "the new" is not a search for new experience, because "the new is what cannot be experienced . . . the Kantian thing-in-itself, the inexperiencible as such" (41).

71. On Baudelaire and the allegorical tradition, see Patrick Labarthe, *Baudelaire et la tradition de l'allégorie* (Geneva: Droz, 1999), esp. chap. 9, "Paris comme décor allégorique," 447–62.

72. "The Dog and the Flask," "A Lost Halo." Many poems in the *Spleen de Paris* have allegorical titles such as "The Gifts of the Fairies," "The Generous Gambler," "The Temptations; or Eros, Plutus and Glory."

73. *Cor.,* 2:254. My translation. Baudelaire's "l'horreur de la face humaine" is, itself, translated from Thomas De Quincey's "the tyranny of the human face."

74. *L'on peut arguer que l'allégorie manifeste une surabondance, qu'elle révèle les multiples "correspondances" dont chaque objet réel est entouré . . . Mais l'argument inverse est également recevable: lorsque, dans notre perception, le réel est incapable de valoir comme tel, il devient nécessaire de le doubler d'un second sens pour empêcher la dissipation de tout sens.* Jean Starobinski, *La mélancolie au miroir: Trois lectures de Baudelaire* (Paris: Julliard, 1989) 74. My translation.

75. *OC,* 1:339; *PP,* 87.

76. "Le reliquat du *Spleen de Paris.*" *OC,* 1:369. My translation.

77. *Toutes ces choses pensent par moi, ou je pense par elles (car dans la grandeur de la rêverie le* moi *se perd vite!). OC,* 1:278.

78. *L'étude du beau est un duel où l'artiste crie de frayeur avant d'être vaincu.* The "terror" of the artist and the metaphor of the duel, also to be found in "Le peintre de la vie modern," provided Benjamin with his key argument for the centrality of shock in the experience of modernity. See Benjamin, "On Some Motifs in Baudelaire," 163–65.

79. To Alfred de Vigny, January 30, 1862 (*Cor.,* 2:223). To Sainte Beuve, February 3, 1862 (*Cor,* 2:229). See also Baudelaire's letter to Henry de la Madelène, November 3, 1864: *Faut-il me remettre au* Spleen de Paris (Poèmes en prose) *et si ce genre d'élucubration vous convient, combien vous faut-il de matière, et quel jour?* In French, an *élucubration* is an idea, system, or thought that is both complicated and unfounded.

80. *Qui est celui de nous qui n'a pas, dans ses jours d'ambition, rêvé le miracle d'une prose poétique . . . assez souple et assez heurtée pour s'adapter aux mouvements lyriques de*

l'âme, aux ondulations de la rêverie, aux soubresauts de la conscience. OC, 1:275–76; *PP,* 30.

81. *C'est en feuilletant, pour la vingtième fois au moins, le fameux* Gaspard de la Nuit, *d'Aloysius Bertrand . . . que l'idée m'est venue de tenter quelque chose d'analogue et d'appliquer à la description de la vie moderne . . . le procédé qu'il avait appliqué à la peinture de la vie ancienne. OC,* 1:275.

82. *Hier, à travers la foule du boulevard, je me sentis frôlé par un Être mystérieux que j'avais toujours désiré connaître, et que je reconnus tout de suite, quoique je ne l'eusse jamais vu. OC,* 1:325; *PP,* 74.

83. *Comme j'arrivais à l'extrémité du faubourg, sous les éclairs du gaz, je sentis un bras qui se coulait doucement sous le mien . . . OC,* 1:353; *PP,* 98.

84. Many of them incorporate the notion of duality in their titles: "The Double Bedroom," "The Soup and the Clouds," "The Savage Woman and the Little Sweetheart," and "Which is the True Benedicta?"

CHAPTER 4

1. The Romantic fascination with mimes and circus artists has been studied by Jean Starobinski in his classic *Portrait de l'artiste en saltimbanque* (Geneva: Skira, 1957). See also Ross Chambers, "The Artist as Performing Dog," *Comparative Literature* 23.4 (1971) 312–24.

2. Modern audiences may remember the plot of this pantomime from Marcel Carné's 1943 masterpiece *Children of Paradise* (*Les Enfants du Paradis*).

3. *La Revue de Paris,* September 4, 1842. In Louis Péricaud, *Le Théâtre des Funambules, ses mimes, ses acteurs et ses pantomimes* (Paris: L. Sapin, 1897) 255. Translation mine.

4. On Jean-Gaspard-Baptiste Deburau and his contribution to the pantomime, see Tristan Rémy, *Jean-Gaspard Deburau* (Paris: L'Arche, 1954); and Adriane Despot,"Jean-Gaspard Deburau and the Pantomime at the Théâtre des Funambules,"*Educational Theater Journal,* vol. 27.3, October 1975, 364–76. On the artistic fortune of Pierrot and the pantomime in nineteenth-century France, see Robert Storey, *Pierrots on the Stage of Desire: Nineteenth Century French Literary Artists and the Comic Pantomime* (Princeton: Princeton UP, 1985) 3–35. Storey emphasizes the diversity and complexity of Pierrot's pantomimes, ranging from the fairy-tale-like *pantomime féérique* to the *pantomime réaliste,* while Despot argues that all pantomimes essentially shared the same "atmosphere of a light, small-scale, nonsensical adventures enlivened with comic dances, ridiculous battles, and confrontations placed in a . . . commonplace setting" (366).

5. Theaters were strictly regulated in the early nineteenth century. In 1807, Napoleon reduced the number of Parisian theaters and restricted the repertoire of each. Napoleon's decree was repealed in 1815, but the restored monarchy maintained the practice of regulating the repertoire and productions of newly opened theaters. The decree that authorized the opening of the Funambules ensured that there would be only acrobatics on the stage. See Marvin Carlson, "The Golden Age of the Boulevard," *Drama Review* 18.1 (1974) 29; and Maurice Albert, *Les théâtres des boulevards* (Paris: Société française d'imprimerie, 1902).

6. . . . *il égrène en scènes muettes, délicieusement lyriques et bouffonnes, les innom-*

brables rhapsodies de son poème. Théodore de Banville, *Mes souvenirs,* in Albert, *Les théâtres des boulevards,* 276.

7. The anecdote was told by Auguste Vitu in *L'Echo,* September 27, 1846; in Bandy and Pichois, *Baudelaire devant ses contemporains,* 173–74.

8. This cohort of distinguished Romantic poets must have seemed out of place amid the crowds that jeered, screeched, and burst into furious applause from the upper rows of the Théâtre des Funambules on the Boulevard du Temple. The theaters and music halls lining the boulevard offered the kinds of entertainment likely to attract a large and varied crowd: vaudevilles, crude comedies accompanied by singing and acrobatics, melodramas (often embellished with song, ballet, and exotic settings), and pantomimes. For a vivid description of the Boulevard du Temple in the early 1800s, see Carlson, "Golden Age of the Boulevard."

9. Gustave Le Vavasseur, quoted by E. Crépet and J. Crépet, *Baudelaire* (Messein, 1906) 56. Another friend, Eugène Prarond, remembered that Baudelaire had attended almost all of Deburau's performances. See E. Prarond and J. Buisson, "Lettres à Eugène Crépet sur la jeunesse de Baudelaire," *Mercure de France,* September 1, 1954, 17.

10. *Le ballet et la pantomime ont le courage de leur opinion: Nous sommes antinaturels, disent-ils . . .* Champfleury, *Souvenirs des Funambules* (Paris: Michel Lévy, 1859) 161.

11. *La pantomime est l'épuration de la comédie; c'en est la quintessence . . . De l'essence du rire. OC,* 2:540.

12. See Storey, *Pierrots,* 29.

13. "The Wild Woman and the Little Sweetheart."

14. *PP,* 43; *OC,* 1:290. The emphasis is Baudelaire's.

15. On this point, see Georges Blin, *Le sadisme de Baudelaire* (Paris: José Corti, 1948). On "A Hero's Death" and the sadism of the prose poems, see Leo Bersani, *Baudelaire and Freud* (Berkeley: U of California P, 1977) 125–36. Bersani reads the poems as evidence of Baudelaire's "psychotic relation to the world" (128) and of his desperate need to protect himself from his self-destructive fantasies. Robert Storey also reads Deburau's pantomimes in a Freudian light. According to him, Pierrot's sadistic pantomimes act out our "wildest fantasies" and most "infantile instincts" (*Pierrots,* 34–35). On "A Hero's Death" and "The Old Acrobat," see also Starobinski, *Portrait de l'artiste en saltimbanque,* 93–99. Starobinski argues that Baudelaire combines two opposed and extreme images of the artist in his portrait of the *saltimbanque,* one of triumph (Fancioulle), the other of degradation (the old acrobat)—ultimately emphasizing the highly precarious status of the artist in society.

16. See *Petits poèmes en prose,* 37. "The Crowds," "The Widows," and "The Old Acrobat" were published together on November 1, 1861, in *La Revue fantaisiste.* Today, they appear, respectively, as poems XII, XIII, and XIV in the collection. All three poems are set in a crowded public place; they form a small unit within the collection.

17. *[Les baraques] se faisaient, en vérité, une concurrence formidable: elles piaillaient, beuglaient, hurlaient. . . . C'était un mélange de cris, de détonations de cuivre, et d'explosions de fusées . . . Il ne criait pas; il ne chantait aucune chanson. . . . Il était muet et im-*

mobile. Mais quel regard profond, inoubliable, il promenait sur la foule et sur ses lumières, dont le flot mouvant s'arrêtait à quelques pas de sa répulsive misère! OC, 295–96; *PP,* 4.

18. *L'observateur est un* prince *qui jouit partout de son incognito. OC,* 2:692.

19. As for the pantomime itself, it never fully recovered from the death of Jean-Gaspard-Baptiste Deburau. In the summer of 1862, the Théâtre des Funambules closed its doors. Later that year, it was destroyed to make way for a new boulevard, the Boulevard du Prince-Eugène, and the entire Boulevard du Temple was razed in Haussmann's redesigning of Paris. The world that inspired Baudelaire's prose poems was being attacked by Haussmann in more ways than one. In 1867, Arsène Houssaye, to whom Baudelaire's prose poems are dedicated, and Théophile Gautier, one of his close friends, had to beg the Baron Haussmann not to throw the remains of Gérard de Nerval out of the cemetery of the Père-Lachaise where the poet had been buried in a temporary lot.

20. *Et, m'en retournant, obsédé par cette vision, je cherchai à analyser ma soudaine douleur, et je me dis: Je viens de voir l'image du vieil homme de lettres qui a survécu à la génération dont il fut le brillant amuseur: du vieux poète sans amis, sans famille, sans enfants, dégradé par sa misère et par l'ingratitude publique, et dans la baraque de qui le monde oublieux ne veut plus entrer! OC,* 1:297; *PP,* 49.

21. See Sonya Stephens's analysis of the divided self in "The Old Mountebank" in *Baudelaire's Prose Poems: The Practice and Politics of Irony* (Oxford: Oxford UP, 1999). Stephens refutes the common critical interpretation that "The Old Mountebank" expresses the poet's defeatism about his art, as she emphasizes the radical separation between the narrator and the acrobat (52–53). In my view, the poem expresses neither defeatism nor optimism, but deceives the reader into believing that it has a moral.

22. *Ces trois visages étaient extraordinairement sérieux, et ces six yeux contemplaient fixement le café nouveau avec une admiration égale. . . . Les yeux du père disaient: "Que c'est beau! Que c'est beau! On dirait que tout l'or du pauvre monde est venu se porter sur ce murs!" Les yeux du petit garçon: "Que c'est beau! Que c'est beau! mais c'est une maison où peuvent seuls entrer les gens qui ne sont pas comme nous." OC,* 1:318; *PP,* 68.

23. For an analysis of the multiple levels of irony in the poem, see Maria Scott, "Superfluous Intrigues in Baudelaire's *Le Spleen de Paris*," *French Studies* 55.3 (2001) 351–62. On the issue of the compatibility between lyricism and irony, a good overview is in Philippe Hamon, "Sujet lyrique et ironie," in *Le sujet lyrique en question,* ed. Dominique Rabaté, Joelle de Sermet, and Yves Vadé (Bordeaux: Presses Universitaires de Bordeaux, 1996) 19–25.

24. *Le premier, parla de Paris en damné quotidien de la capitale . . .* Jules Laforgue, "Notes sur Baudelaire," in *Mélanges posthumes,* 111.

25. "The Widows," *OC,* 1:292.

26. "The Double Bedroom," *OC,* 1:261. My translation.

27. "Les contes de Champfleury," *OC,* 2:21–24; "Les Misérables par Victor Hugo," April 1862, *OC,* 2:217–24.

28. "Mon coeur mis à nu," *OC,* 1:679.

29. On Baudelaire's response to urban poverty, revolution, and social ills, see Edward Ahearn, *Urban Confrontations in Literature and Social Science, 1848–2001* (Farnham: Ashgate, 2010) 26–47; and Richard Burton, *Baudelaire and the Second Republic* (Oxford: Clarendon P, 1991).

30. See Jacques Lacan, *Le Séminaire*, vol. 9 (*Les quatre concepts fondamentaux de la psychanalyse*), ed. J.-A. Miller (Paris: Seuil, 1973) 94–96, 102–3. Lacan argues that all of painting is a way of deceiving (*tromper*) the eye. We are never looking at what we think we are looking at when we look at a picture. In a sense, the trompe-l'oeil exemplifies the deception of all art. The particular seduction of the trompe-l'oeil, according to Lacan, comes with the realization that the painting is something else from what we thought (*autre chose que ce qu'il se donnait*).

31. *OC,* 2:224.

32. *Ce livre est immonde et inepte.* To his mother, August 10, 1862. *Cor.,* 2 :254.

33. *Ce sont des horreurs et des monstruosités qui feraient avorter vos lectrices enceintes.* Letter to Louis Marcelin, February 15, 1865 (*Cor.,* 2:465).

34. *Je me trouve fort à l'aise sous ma* flétrissure, *et je sais que désormais, dans quelque genre de littérature que je me répande, je resterai un monstre et un loup-garou. Cor.,* 1:598. The word *flétrissure* was commonly applied to the branding of criminals and prostitutes in the French justice system before the Revolution.

35. Breton anthologized and introduced "The Bad Glazier" in his *Anthologie de l'humour noir* (Paris: Pauvert, 1966) 133–39. For Sartre's reading of "The Bad Glazier," see *Baudelaire* (Paris: Gallimard, 1963) 39–41.

36. He did not spare even his own friend Arsène Houssaye, to whom *Le Spleen de Paris* is dedicated. Houssaye was himself the author of a sentimental prose poem about a Parisian glazier, in which the desperate man, just as he was about to faint from hunger, is rewarded for his stoicism with a glass of wine and the gift of fraternity. Baudelaire appears to compliment Houssaye for his "Song of the Glazier" in the dedication of the *Petits poèmes en prose.* But if Houssaye had been a more perceptive reader of his friend, he would have been deeply insulted by Baudelaire's homage. See *Petits poèmes en prose,* 180.

37. Benjamin, *The Arcades Project,* 465–66 (J 80, 1).

38. "Morale du joujou," *OC,* 1:582. The essay was first published in 1853.

39. . . . *cet ouvrage tenant à la fois de la vis et du kaléidoscope. OC,* 1:365.

40. *OC,* 2:692.

41. See Georges Potonniée, *Daguerre peintre et décorateur,* Paris, 1935. Reproduced in facsimile in *The Prehistory of Photography: Five Texts,* ed. R. Sobieszek (New York: Arno P, 1979). On Daguerre and the diorama, see also Germain Pabst, "Essai sur l'histoire des panoramas et des dioramas," Paris, 1891, in the same collection. On the diorama and the kaleidoscope, see Crary, *Techniques of the Observer,* 112–16.

42. *Je désire être ramené vers les dioramas dont la magie brutale et énorme sait m'imposer une utile illusion. Je préfère contempler quelques décors de théâtre, où je trouve artistement exprimés et tragiquement concentrés mes rêves les plus chers.* "Le Paysage," in "Salon de 1859," *OC,* 2:668. My translation.

43. The relatively high entrance price of three francs did not stand in the way of the diorama's popularity, but rather was the surest sign of it.

44. In his book on *Romantic Paris,* the art historian Richard Marrinan argues that the craze for the diorama reflected a radical shift in the perception of nature: "The goal was no longer to dominate nature, but to become lost in it." The spectators at the diorama felt the visceral thrill of looking at a landscape "without

a superstructure of rational control." Richard Marrinan, *Romantic Paris* (Stanford: Stanford UP, 2009) 211.

45. Quoted by Potonniée, op. cit., *Daguerre peintre et decorateur,* 54.

46. *OC,* 1:342; *PP,* 90.

47. *Elle est bien laide. Elle est délicieuse pourtant! . . . Elle est fourmi, araignée, si vous voulez, squelette même; mais aussi elle est breuvage, magistère, sorcellerie! En somme, elle est exquise. OC,* 1:343; *PP,* 90. Translation modified.

48. Exceptions are "The Beautiful Dorothea," and, as we will discuss later, the tall widow in "The Widows."

49. "Le public moderne et la photographie," *OC,* 2:617.

50. *. . . si noble dans tout son air que je n'ai pas souvenir d'avoir vu sa pareille dans les collections des aristocratiques beautés du passé. OC,* 1:294.

51. *OC,* 1:355.

52. "L'école païenne," *OC,* 2:49.

53. *Vous ressemblez au public, à qui il ne faut jamais présenter des parfums délicats qui l'exaspèrent, mais des ordures soigneusement choisies.* "The Dog and the Flask." *OC,* 1:284.

54. *En littérature, [le Français] est scatophage. Il raffole des excréments.* "Mon cœur mis à nu," 34, *OC,* 1:698.

55. *Pauvre Belgique, OC,* 2:831. *Un jeune écrivain [Stéphane Mallarmé] a récemment eu une conception ingénieuse, mais non absolument juste. Le monde va finir. . . . Un Barnum de l'avenir montre aux hommes dégradés de son temps une belle femme des âges anciens artificiellement conservée. 'Eh quoi! disent-ils, l'humanité a pu être aussi belle que cela?' Je dis que cela n'est pas vrai. L'homme dégradé s'admirerait et appellerait la beauté laideur. Voyez les déplorables Belges.*

56. *Pauvre Belgique, OC,* 2:843, *feuillet* 69; also *feuillet* 71: "The man who makes himself wealthy at fun-fairs by eating dogs while they are still alive. An audience (*public*) of women and children."

CONCLUSION

1. Siegfried Giedion, *Space, Time, and Architecture* (Cambridge: Harvard UP, 1962) 676. The book originally came out in 1941. Giedion's ideas on urbanism strongly influenced American city planners, most notably Robert Moses.

2. See ibid., 674.

3. *O Créateur! Peut-il exister des monstres aux yeux de Celui-là seul qui sait pourquoi ils existent, comment ils se sont faits, et comment ils auraient pu ne pas se faire? OC,* 1:356; *PP,* 101. Translation modified. The emphasis is Baudelaire's.

4. *Il me serait d'ailleurs impossible de dire pourquoi je fus pris à l'égard de ce pauvre homme d'une haine aussi soudaine que despotique. PP,* 38; *OC,* 1:286. Translation modified.

5. *Singulière vision!* "A coup sûr, me dis-je, cette pauvreté-là, si pauvreté il y a, ne doit pas admettre l'économie sordide; un si noble visage m'en répond. Pourquoi donc reste-t-elle volontairement dans un milieu où elle fait une tache si éclatante?" Mais en passant curieusement auprès d'elle, je crus en deviner la raison. La grande veuve tenait par la main un enfant comme elle vêtu de noir; si modique que fut le prix d'entrée, ce prix suffisait

peut-être pour payer un des besoins du petit être, mieux encore, une superfluité, un jouet.
OC, 1:294; *PP,* 47.

6. *OC,* 1:324; *PP,* 73. *Mais dans mon misérable cerveau, toujours occupé à chercher
midi à quatorze heures . . . entra soudainement cette idée qu'une pareille conduite, de la
part de mon ami, n'était excusable que par le désir de créer un événement dans la vie de ce
pauvre diable, peut-être même de connaître les conséquences diverses, funestes ou autres, que
peut engendrer une pièce fausse dans la main d'un mendiant. Ne pouvait-elle pas se mul-
tiplier en pièces vraies? Ne pouvait-elle pas aussi le conduire en prison? Un cabaretier, un
boulanger, par exemple, allaient peut-être le faire arrêter comme faux-monnayeur ou*
comme propagateur de fausse monnaie. *Tout aussi bien la pièce fausse serait peut-
être, pour un pauvre petit spéculateur, le germe d'une richesse de quelques jours. Et ainsi ma
fantaisie allait son train, prêtant des ailes à l'esprit de mon ami et tirant toutes les déduc-
tions possibles de toutes les hypothèses possibles.*

7. Jacques Derrida, *Given Time I: Counterfeit Money,* trans. Peggy Kamuf
(Chicago: U of Chicago P, 1992) 119–20.

8. Ibid., 121–22.

9. *La vie multiple et la grâce mouvante de tous les éléments de la vie. OC,* 2:692.

10. *. . . tuer le Temps. Tuer ce monstre-là, n'est-ce pas l'occupation la plus ordinaire
et la plus légitime de chacun?* "The Gallant Marksman," *OC,* 1:349; *PP,* 96. Translation modified.

11. "Our Old Feuillage," "Give Me the Splendid Silent Sun."

12. Brown and Rubin, *Whitman of the Aurora,* 45.

13. Ibid., 26.

14. *LG,* 308–9.

15. Augustine, *Confessions,* XI: 20.26, trans. R. S. Pine-Coffin (Harmondsworth: Penguin, 1961) 269. My discussion of Augustine on time is in-
debted to the unpublished dissertation by George Katsaros, "Tragedy, Catharsis,
and Reason: An Essay on the Idea of the Tragic," Yale University, Department of
Comparative Literature, 2002.

16. See Walter Benjamin's diagnosis of the crisis of lyric poetry in his essay
"On Some Motifs in Baudelaire."

17. William Watts translates *contuitus* as "our sight" (Cambridge: Loeb Classical Library, Harvard UP, 1912); Pierre de Labriolle, "la vision directe," in *Les
confessions,* 2 vols. (Paris: Belles-Lettres, 1926); R. S. Pine-Coffin, "direct perception"; and Henry Chadwick, "immediate awareness" (Oxford: Oxford UP, 1991).
The *Oxford Latin Dictionary, s.v. contueor* 1.c, has "to contemplate mentally." Close
to and perhaps deriving from Augustine's usage is the definition of *contuitus*
from the *Dictionary of Medieval Latin from British Sources,* "contemplation, (spiritual) vision." The bracketing of the adjective "spiritual" shows, again, the irreducible ambiguity of the term.

18. See Labriolle: *Le mot contuitus ne se rencontre pas avant l'ère chrétienne. Il
signifie 1) l'acte de regarder 2) la vue directe, la contemplation spirituelle* (Augustine, *Les
confessions,* 2:341).

Bibliography

Agamben, Giorgio. *Infancy and History*. Trans. Liz Heron. London: Verso, 1993.

Ahearn, Edward. *Urban Confrontations in Literature and Social Science, 1848–2001*. Farnham: Ashgate, 2010.

Albert, Maurice. *Les théâtres des boulevards*. Paris: Société française d'imprimerie, 1902.

Allen, Gay Wilson. *The Solitary Singer: A Critical Biography of Walt Whitman*. Chicago: U of Chicago P, 1955.

Aristotle. *Poetics*. Trans. Richard Janko. Indianapolis: Hackett, 1987.

Asselineau, Roger. "When Walt Whitman Was a Parisian." *Mickle Street Review* 9.2 (1988): 30–34.

Augustine. *Confessions*. Trans. Henry Chadwick. Oxford: Oxford UP, 1991.

Augustine. *Les confessions*. 2 vols. Trans. P. de Labriolle. Paris: Les Belles-Lettres, 1926.

Augustine. *Confessions*. Trans. R. S. Pine-Coffin. Harmondsworth: Penguin, 1961.

Augustine. *Confessions*. Trans. William Watts. 2 vols. Cambridge: Loeb Classical Library, 1912.

Bandy, W. T. "Whitman and Baudelaire." *Walt Whitman Quarterly Review* 1.3 (1983) 53–55.

Bandy, W. T., and Claude Pichois. *Baudelaire devant ses contemporains*. Monaco: Editions du Rocher, 1957.

Baudelaire, Charles. *Correspondance*. Ed. Claude Pichois and Jean Ziegler. 2 vols. Paris: Gallimard/Bibliothèque de la Pléiade, 1973.

Baudelaire, Charles. *Curiosités esthétiques et l'art romantique*. Ed. Henri Lemaître. Paris: Garnier, 1962.

Baudelaire, Charles. *The Essence of Laughter and Other Essays, Journals and Letters*. Ed. and trans. Peter Quennell. New York: Meridian Books, 1956.

Baudelaire, Charles. *The Flowers of Evil*. Ed. Marthiel Mathews and Jackson Mathews. New York: New Directions, 1963.

Baudelaire, Charles. *The Flowers of Evil*. Trans. Keith Waldrop. Middletown, Conn.: Wesleyan UP, 2006.

Baudelaire, Charles. *Intimate Journals*. Trans. Christopher Isherwood. Hollywood: Marcel Rodd, 1947.

Baudelaire, Charles. *Oeuvres complètes*. Ed. Claude Pichois. 2 vols. Paris: Galli-
    mard/Bibliothèque de la Pléiade, 1975.

Baudelaire, Charles. *Paris Spleen: Little Poems in Prose*. Trans. Keith Waldrop. Mid-
    dletown, Conn.: Wesleyan UP, 2009.

Baudelaire, Charles. *Petits Poèmes en prose*. Ed. Robert Kopp. Paris: José Corti, 1969.

Baudelaire, Charles. *Petits Poèmes en prose (Le Spleen de Paris)*. Ed. Henri Lemaître.
    Paris: Classiques Garnier, 1962.

Baudelaire, Charles. *Poems of Baudelaire: A Translation of "Les Fleurs du Mal."* Trans.
    Roy Campbell. New York: Pantheon, 1962.

Baudelaire, Charles. *The Prose Poems and La Fanfarlo*. Trans. Rosemary Lloyd. New
    York: Oxford UP, 1991.

Baudelaire, Charles. *Selected Writings on Art and Literature*. Trans. P. E. Charvet.
    Harmondsworth: Penguin, 1972.

Baudelaire Petit Palais, 23 novembre 1968–17 mars 1969. Paris: Réunion des musées
    nationaux, 1969.

Barnum, P[hineas] T[aylor]. *Struggles and Triumphs*. 1869. Harmondsworth: Pen-
    guin, 1981.

Benjamin, Walter. *The Arcades Project*. Trans. Howard Eiland and Kevin McLaugh-
    lin. Cambridge: Belknap P of Harvard UP, 1999.

Benjamin, Walter. *Charles Baudelaire: A Lyric Poet in the High Era of Capitalism*.
    Trans. Harry Zohn. London: Verso, 1983.

Benjamin, Walter. *Charles Baudelaire: Un poète lyrique à l'apogée du capitalisme*.
    Trans. Jean Lacoste. Paris: Petite Bibliothèque Payot, 2002.

Benjamin, Walter. *Das Passagen-Werk*. In *Gesammelte Schriften*. Ed. Rolf Tiede-
    mann. Vol. 5, 1. Frankfurt: Suhrkamp Verlag, 1982.

Benjamin, Walter. "On Some Motifs in Baudelaire." *Illuminations*. Trans. H.
    Zohn. Ed. Hannah Arendt. New York: Schocken Books, 1969. 155–200.

Benjamin, Walter. *Paris Capitale du dix-neuvième Siècle: Le livre des passages*. Trans.
    Jean Lacoste. 3d ed. Paris: Editions du Cerf, 1997.

Benjamin, Walter. "Zentralpark." In *Gesammelte Schriften*. Ed. Rolf Tiedemann.
    Vol. I, 2. Frankfurt am Main: Suhrkamp Verlag, 1982.

Benson, Eugene. "Charles Baudelaire Poet of the Malign." *Atlantic Monthly*, Feb-
    ruary 1869, 171–77.

Bernard, Suzanne. *Le poème en prose de Baudelaire jusqu'à nos jours*. Paris: Librarie
    Nizet, 1959.

Bersani, Leo. *Baudelaire and Freud*. Berkeley: U of California P, 1977.

Bertolini, Vincent J. "Hinting and Reminding: The Rhetoric of Performative Em-
    bodiment in *Leaves of Grass*." *ELH* 69.4 (2002) 1047–82.

Blin, Georges. *Le sadisme de Baudelaire*. Paris: José Corti, 1948.

Bloom, Harold. "'To the Tally of My Soul': Whitman's Image of Voice." *The Or-
    dering Mirror: Readers and Context*. New York: Fordham UP, 1993. 42–63.

Boyer, M. Christine. *The City of Collective Memory: Its Historical Imagery and Architec-
    tural Entertainments*. Cambridge: MIT P, 1994.

Brand, Dana. "'Immense Phantom Concourse': Whitman and the Urban
    Crowd." *The Spectator and the City in Nineteenth Century Literature*. Cambridge:
    Cambridge UP, 1991. 156–85.

Brasher, Thomas L. *Whitman as Editor of the "Brooklyn Daily Eagle."* Detroit: Wayne State UP, 1970.

Breton, André. *Anthologie de l'humour noir.* Paris: Pauvert, 1966.

Brown, Charles H., and Joseph Jay Rubin, eds. *Walt Whitman of the "New York Aurora."* Carrolltown, Pennsylvania: Bald Eagle P, 1950.

Burke, Edmund. *A Philosophical Enquiry into the Origins of Our Ideas of the Sublime and the Beautiful.* 1757. Oxford: Oxford UP, 1990.

Burns, Richard, and James Sanders. *New York: An Illustrated History.* New York: Knopf, 1999.

Burroughs, John. *Notes on Walt Whitman as a Poet and Person.* In *Critical Essays on Walt Whitman.* Ed. James Woodress. Boston: G. K. Hall, 1983. 94–98.

Burton, Richard. *Baudelaire and the Second Republic: Writing and Revolution.* Oxford: Clarendon P, 1991.

Cairns, W. B. "Swinburne's Opinion of Whitman." *American Literature* 3.2 (1931) 125–35.

Carlson, Marvin. "The Golden Age of the Boulevard." *Drama Review* 18.1 (1974) 25–33.

Caws, Mary-Ann, and Hermine Riffatterre, eds. *The Prose Poem in France: Theory and Practice.* New York: Columbia UP, 1983.

Chambers, Ross. "The Artist as Performing Dog." *Comparative Literature* 23.4 (1971) 312–24.

Chambers, Ross. "Heightening the Lowly: Baudelaire's 'Je n'ai pas oublié . . .' and 'À une passante.'" *Nineteenth-Century French Studies* 37.1–2 (2008) 42–51.

Chambers, Ross. "Trois Paysages urbains: Les poèmes liminaires des 'Tableaux parisiens.'" *Modern Philology* 80.4 (1983) 372–89.

Champfleury (Jules Husson-Fleury). *Souvenirs des Funambules.* Paris: Michel Lévy, 1859.

Chevalier, Louis. *The Assassination of Paris.* Trans. E. Jordan. Chicago: U of Chicago P, 1994.

Clark, T. J. *The Painting of Modern Life: Paris in the Art of Manet and His Followers.* Rev. ed. Princeton: Princeton UP, 1999.

Clarke, Graham. *Walt Whitman: The Poem as Private History.* New York: St. Martin's P, 1991.

Clements, Patricia. "'Strange Flowers': Some Notes on the Baudelaire of Swinburne and Pater." *Modern Language Review* 76.1 (1981) 20–30.

Coffmann, Stanley. "'Crossing Brooklyn Ferry': A Note on the Catalogue Technique in Whitman's Poetry." *Modern Philology* 51.4 (1954) 225–32.

Collot, Michel. *La poésie moderne et la structure d'horizon.* Paris: PUF, 1989.

Collot, Michel. "Le sujet lyrique hors de soi." *Figures du sujet lyrique.* Ed. Dominique Rabaté. Paris: PUF, 1996. 113–25.

Compagnon, Antoine. *Les anti-modernes, de Joseph de Maistre à Roland Barthes.* Paris: Gallimard, 2005.

Compagnon, Antoine. *Baudelaire devant l'innombrable.* Paris: Presses de l'Université Paris-Sorbonne, 2003.

Conrad, Peter. *The Art of the City: Views and Versions of New York.* New York: Oxford UP, 1984.

Crary, Jonathan. "Spectacle, Attention, Counter-Memory." *October* 50 (Autumn 1989) 96–107.

Crary, Jonathan. *Techniques of the Observer: On Vision and Modernity in the Nineteenth Century.* Cambridge: MIT P, 1990.

Crépet, Eugène, and Jacques Crépet. *Baudelaire.* Messein, 1906.

Cutler, Ed. "Passage to Modernity: *Leaves of Grass* and the 1853 Crystal Palace Exhibition in New York." *Walt Whitman Quarterly Review* 16.2 (1998) 65–89.

Davis, Keith F. *The Origins of American Photography: From Daguerreotype to Dry-Plate, 1839–1885.* New Haven: Yale UP, 2008.

De Kuyper, Eric, and Emile Poppe. "Voir et regarder." *Communications* 34 (1981) 85–96.

De Man, Paul. "Literary History and Literary Modernity." *Blindness and Insight.* Rev. ed. Minneapolis: U of Minnesota P, 1983.

Derrida, Jacques. *Given Time I: Counterfeit Money.* Trans. Peggy Kamuf. Chicago: U of Chicago P, 1992.

Despot, Adriane. "Jean-Gaspard Deburau and the Pantomime at the Théâtre des Funambules." *Educational Theater Journal* 27.3 (1975): 364–76.

Dickens, Charles. *American Notes and Pictures from Italy.* 1842. New York: Macmillan, 1903.

Dimock, Wai Chee. "Whitman, Syntax, and Political Theory." *Breaking Bounds: Whitman and American Cultural Studies.* Ed. Betsy Erkkila and Jay Grossman. New York: Oxford UP, 1996. 62–79.

Dougherty, James. *Walt Whitman and the Citizen's Eye.* Baton Rouge: Louisiana State UP, 1993.

Douglas, Ann. *The Feminization of American Culture.* New York: Avon P, 1977.

Douglas, Ann. *Terrible Honesty: Mongrel Manhattan in the 1920s.* New York: Farrar, Straus and Giroux, 1995.

Du Camp, Maxime. *Paris, ses organes, ses fonctions, et sa vie dans la seconde moitié du dix-neuvième siècle.* 6 vols. Paris, 1883.

Duhamel, Georges. *America the Menace: Scenes from the Life of the Future.* Trans. C. Thompson. Boston: Houghton Mifflin, 1931.

Eliot, T[homas] S[tearns]. "Baudelaire." 1930. *Selected Essays.* Rev. ed. New York: Harcourt, Brace, 1953.

Eliot, T[homas] S[tearns]. *From Poe to Valéry: A Lecture Delivered at the Library of Congress on Friday, November 19, 1948.* Washington, D.C.: Library of Congress, 1949.

Eliot, T[homas] S[tearns]. Introduction. *Selected Poems of Ezra Pound.* London: Faber and Gwyer, 1928.

Eliot, T[homas] S[tearns]. Rev. of *Whitman: An Interpretation in Narrative,* by Emory Holloway. *The Nation and Atheneum,* December 18, 1926, 426.

Erkkila, Betsy. *Walt Whitman among the French: Poet and Myth.* Princeton: Princeton UP, 1980.

Erkkila, Betsy. "Whitman and the Homosexual Republic." *Walt Whitman: The Centennial Essays.* Ed. Ed Folsom. Iowa City: U of Iowa P, 1994. 153–71.

Erkkila, Betsy, and Jay Grossman, eds. *Breaking Bounds: Whitman and American Cultural Studies.* New York: Oxford UP, 1996.

Etienne, Louis. "Walt Whitman, philosophe et 'rowdy.'" *La revue européenne*, November 1861, 104–17.

Eugny, Anne, and René Coursaget, eds. *Au temps de Baudelaire, Guys et Nadar.* Paris: Les Editions du Chêne, 1945.

Farland, Maria. "Decomposing City: Walt Whitman's New York and the Science of Life and Death." *ELH* 74.4 (2007) 799–827.

Ferguson, Priscilla Parkhurst. *Paris as Revolution: Writing the Nineteenth-Century City.* Berkeley: U of California P, 1994.

Flaubert, Gustave. *Correspondance.* Ed. Bernard Masson. Paris: Gallimard/Folio, 1998.

Folsom, Ed, ed. *Walt Whitman: The Centennial Essays.* Iowa City: U of Iowa P, 1994.

Foster, George G. *New York by Gas-Light and Other Urban Sketches.* 1850. Ed. Stuart Blumin. Berkeley: U of California P, 1990.

Foucault, Michel. *Discipline and Punish: The Birth of the Prison.* Trans. Alan Sheridan. New York: Pantheon Books, 1979.

Fountain, Lucy (Kate Hillard). "Charles Pierre Baudelaire." *Lippincott's Magazine* 8 (October 1871) 383–88.

Fournel, Victor. *Paris nouveau et Paris futur.* Paris: J. Lecoffre, 1865.

Giedion, Siegfried. *Space, Time, and Architecture.* Cambridge: Harvard UP, 1962.

Gilbert, Roger. "From Anxiety to Power: Grammar and Crisis in 'Crossing Brooklyn Ferry.'" *Nineteenth Century Literature* 42.3 (1987) 339–61.

Godhes, Clarence. "Whitman as 'One of the Roughs.'" *Walt Whitman Review* 8 (March 1962). Rpt. in *Walt Whitman: Critical Assessments.* Vol. 4. Mountfield, East Sussex: Helm Information, 1995. 430–31.

Goncourt, Jules de, and Edmond de Goncourt. *Journal: Mémoires de la vie littéraire.* Vol. 1. Paris: R. Laffont, 1989.

Guerrero, Gustavo. *Poétique et poésie lyrique.* Trans. G. Guerrero and A.-J. Stéphan. Paris: Seuil, 2002.

Hamon, Philippe. *Imageries: Littérature et image au dix-neuvième siècle.* Paris: José Corti, 2001.

Hamon, Philippe. "Sujet lyrique et ironie." *Le sujet lyrique en question.* Ed. Dominique Rabaté, Joelle de Sermet, Yves Vadé. Bordeaux: Presses Universitaires de Bordeaux, 1996.

Hazan, Eric. *L'invention de Paris.* Paris: Seuil, 2002.

Higonnet, Patrice. *Paris, Capital of the World.* Trans. Arthur Goldhammer. Cambridge: Belknap P, 2002.

Hollis, C. Carroll. *Language and Style in "Leaves of Grass."* Baton Rouge: Louisiana State UP, 1983.

James, Henry. "Charles Baudelaire." 1878. *French Poets and Novelists.* London: Macmillan, 1904. 57–65.

James, William. *Talks to Teachers on Psychology and to Students on Some of Life's Ideals.* New York: Holt, 1899.

Johnson, Barbara. *Défigurations du langage poétique: La seconde révolution baudelairienne.* Paris: Flammarion, 1979.

Jones, Colin. *Paris: Biography of a City.* New York: Viking, 2004.

Kammen, Michael. *Colonial New York.* New York: KTO P, 1975.

Katsaros, George. "Tragedy, Catharsis, and Reason: An Essay on the Idea of the Tragic." Diss. Yale University, 2002.

Killingsworth, M. Jimmie. "Whitman's Physical Eloquence." *Walt Whitman: The Centennial Essays.* Ed. Ed Folsom. Iowa City: U of Iowa P, 1994. 68–78.

Killingsworth, M. Jimmie. *Whitman's Poetry of the Body: Sexuality, Politics, and the Text.* Chapel Hill: U of North Carolina P, 1979.

Koolhaas, Rem. *Delirious New York: A Retroactive Manifesto for Manhattan.* New York: Monacelli P, 1994.

Labarthe, Patrick. *Baudelaire et la tradition de l'allégorie.* Geneva: Droz, 1999.

Lacan, Jacques. *Le Séminaire.* Vol. 9. Ed. J.-A. Miller. Paris: Seuil, 1973.

Laforgue, Jules. "Notes sur Baudelaire." *Mélanges posthumes.* Paris: Mercure de France, 1903. 111–18.

Lalor, Gene. "Whitman Among the New York Literary Bohemians: 1859–1862." *Walt Whitman Review* 25.4 (1979) 131–47.

Lawrence, D[avid] H[erbert]. *Studies in Classic American Literature.* 1922. New York: Doubleday, 1959.

Le Corbusier (Charles-Edouard Jeanneret-Gris). *The City of Tomorrow and its Planning.* Trans. Frederick Etchells. London: J. Rotker, 1929.

Lefebvre, Henri. *La révolution urbaine.* Paris: Gallimard, 1970.

Loving, Jerome. "'Broadway, the Magnificent!' A Newly Discovered Whitman Essay." *Walt Whitman Quarterly Review* 12.4 (1995) 209–16.

Loving, Jerome. *Walt Whitman: The Song of Himself.* Berkeley: U of California P, 1999.

MacLean, Marie. *Narrative as Performance: The Baudelairean Experiment.* London: Routledge, 1988.

McDonough, Tom. *Guy Debord and the Situationist International.* Cambridge: MIT P, 2002.

Marchand, Bernard. *Paris: Histoire d'une ville.* Paris: Seuil/Histoire, 1993.

Marder, Elissa. *Dead Time: Temporal Disorders in the Wake of Modernity.* Stanford: Stanford UP, 2001.

Marrinan, Richard. *Romantic Paris: Histories of a Cultural Landscape, 1800–1850.* Stanford: Stanford UP, 2009.

Martin, Robert K. *The Homosexual Tradition in American Poetry.* Austin: U of Texas P, 1979.

Matthiessen, F. O. *American Renaissance: Art and Expression in the Age of Emerson and Whitman.* New York: Oxford UP, 1941.

Maulpoix, Jean-Michel. *La poésie comme l'amour: Essai sur la relation lyrique.* Paris: Mercure de France, 1998.

Maulpoix, Jean-Michel. "La quatrième personne du singulier: Esquisse de portrait du sujet lyrique moderne." *Figures du sujet lyrique.* Ed. Dominique Rabaté. Paris: PUF, 1996. 147–60.

McGinnis, Reginald. *La prostitution sacrée: Essai sur Baudelaire.* Paris: Belin, coll. "L'extrême contemporain," 1994.

Meisel, Martin. *Realizations: Narrative, Pictorial and Theatrical Arts in Nineteenth Century England.* Princeton: Princeton UP, 1983.

Meschonnic, Henri. *Critique du rythme: Anthropologie historique du langage.* La Grasse: Verdier, 1982.

Meschonnic, Henri. *Les états de la poétique.* Paris: PUF, 1985.

Meyers, Terry L. "Swinburne and Whitman: Further Evidence." *Walt Whitman Quarterly Review* 14.1 (1996) 1–11.

Miyoshi, Masao. *As We Saw Them: The First Japanese Embassy to the United States.* Berkeley: U of California P, 1979.

Moon, Michael. *Disseminating Whitman: Revision and Corporeality in "Leaves of Grass."* Cambridge: Harvard UP, 1991.

Morizet, André. *Du vieux Paris au Paris moderne: Haussmann et ses prédécesseurs.* Paris: Hachette, 1932.

Mumford, Lewis. *The City in History: Its Origins, Its Transformations, and Its Prospects.* New York: Harcourt Brace, 1961.

Myerson, Joel, ed. *Whitman in his own Time.* Iowa City: U of Iowa P, 1991.

Nadar (Félix Tournachon). *Charles Baudelaire intime.* 1911. Neuchâtel: Ides et Calendes/La Bibliothèque des Arts, 1994.

Newmark, Kevin. "Off the Charts: Walter Benjamin's Depiction of Baudelaire." *Baudelaire and the Poetics of Modernity.* Ed. Patricia Ward. Nashville: Vanderbilt UP, 2001. 72–84.

O'Connor, William. *The Good Gray Poet: A Vindication.* In *Critical Essays on Walt Whitman.* Ed. James Woodress. Boston: G. K. Hall, 1983. 50–55.

O'Neill, Eugene. *Long Day's Journey Into Night.* Rev. ed. New Haven: Yale UP, 1989.

Oppen, George. *Collected Poems.* New York: New Directions, 1975.

Parker, Simon. "Unrhymed Modernity: New York City, the Popular Newspaper Page, and the Forms of Whitman's Poetry." *Walt Whitman Quarterly Review* 16.3–4 (1999) 161–71.

Péricaud, Louis. *Le théâtre des Funambules, ses mimes, ses acteurs et ses pantomimes.* Paris: Sapin, 1897.

Photographier l'architecture, 1851–1920. Paris: Collection du Musée des Monuments français, 1994.

Pichois, Claude. *Baudelaire: Etudes et témoignages.* Neuchâtel: La Baconnière, 1967.

Pichois, Claude, and Jean-Paul Avice, eds. *Baudelaire Paris.* Paris: Editions Paris Musées/Quai Voltaire, 1994.

Pichois, Claude, and François Ruchon, eds. *Baudelaire: Documents iconographiques.* Geneva: Pierre Cailler, 1960.

Pichois, Claude, and Jean Ziegler. *Charles Baudelaire.* 2nd ed. Paris: Fayard, 1996.

Pinkney, David H. *Napoleon III and the Rebuilding of Paris.* Princeton: Princeton UP, 1968.

Poe, Edgar Allan. *Doings of Gotham.* Ed. T. Olive Mabbot. Pottsville: Jacob E. Spannuth, 1929.

Poe, Edgar Allan. "The Man of the Crowd." *Poetry and Tales.* Ed. Patrick McQuinn. New York: Library of America, 1984. 388–96.

Poggenburg, Raymond P. *Charles Baudelaire, une micro-histoire.* Paris: José Corti, 1987.

Poulet, Georges. *Etudes sur le temps humain.* Vol. 3. Paris: Plon, 1964.

Poulet, Georges. *Exploding Poetry: Baudelaire/Rimbaud.* Trans. Françoise Meltzer. Chicago: U of Chicago P, 1984.

Pound, Ezra. *ABC of Reading.* 1934. New York: New Directions, 1960.

Pound, Ezra. "What I Feel About Walt Whitman." In *Critical Essays on Walt Whitman.* Ed. James Woodress. Boston: G. K. Hall, 1983. 191–92.

Rabaté, Dominique. "Enonciation poétique, énonciation lyrique." *Figures du sujet lyrique.* Ed. Dominique Rabaté. Paris: PUF, 1996. 65–79.

Rabaté, Dominique. *Poétiques de la voix.* Paris: José Corti, 1999.

Rabaté, Dominique, Joelle de Sermet, and Yves Vadé, eds. *Le sujet lyrique en question.* Bordeaux: Presses Universitaires de Bordeaux, 1996.

Réau, Louis, et al. *L'Oeuvre du baron Haussmann, Préfet de la Seine.* Paris: PUF, 1954.

Reinach, Adolphe. *Textes grecs et latins relatifs à l'histoire de la peinture ancienne.* Paris: C. Klincksieck, 1921.

Rémy, Tristan. *Jean-Gaspard Deburau.* Paris: L'Arche, 1954.

Reynolds, David. *Walt Whitman's America: A Cultural Biography.* New York: Random House, 1996.

Rice, Shelley. *Parisian Views.* Cambridge: MIT P, 1987.

Robertson, Michael. *Worshipping Walt: The Whitman Disciples.* Princeton: Princeton UP, 2008.

Roger, Philippe. *The American Enemy: A Story of French Anti-Americanism.* Trans. S. Bowman. Chicago: U of Chicago P, 2005.

Rouillard, Dominique. "L'Amérique n'a pas de monuments." *Américanisme et modernité: L'idéal américain dans l'architecture.* Ed. Jean-Louis Cohen and Hubert Damisch. Paris: Presses de l'EHESS, 1993. 51–74.

Sante, Luc. *Low Life: Lures and Snares of Old New York.* New York: Farrar, Straus and Girox, 2003.

Sartre, Jean-Paul. *Baudelaire.* Paris: Gallimard, 1963.

Schneider, Michel. *Baudelaire: Les années profondes.* Paris: Seuil, coll. "Librarie du XXe siècle," 1994.

Scott, Maria. "Superfluous Intrigues in Baudelaire's Prose Poems." *French Studies* 55.3 (2001) 351–62.

Selincourt, Basil de. *Walt Whitman: A Critical Study.* 1914. New York: Russell and Russell, 1964.

Sharpe, William C. *Unreal Cities: Urban Figuration in Wordsworth, Baudelaire, Whitman, Eliot, and Williams.* Baltimore: Johns Hopkins UP, 1990.

Sharpe, William C., ed. *Walt Whitman: Critical Assessments.* 4 vols. Mountfield, East Sussex: Helm Information, 1995.

Siegel, Adrienne. *The Image of the American City in Popular Literature, 1820–1870.* Port Washington, N.Y.: Kennikat P, 1981.

Sobieszek, R., ed. *The Prehistory of Photography: Five Texts.* New York: Arno P, 1979.

Spann, Edward K. *The New Metropolis: New York City, 1840–1857.* New York: Columbia UP, 1981.

Stansell, Christine. "Whitman at Pfaff's: Commercial Culture, Literary Life and New York Bohemia at Mid-Century." *Walt Whitman Quarterly Review* 10.3 (1993) 107–26.

Starobinski, Jean. *La mélancolie au miroir: Trois lectures de Baudelaire.* Paris: Julliard, 1989.

Starobinski, Jean. *Portrait de l'artiste en saltimbanque.* Geneva: Skira, 1957.

Stephens, Sonya. *Baudelaire's Prose Poems: The Practice and Politics of Irony.* Oxford: Oxford UP, 1999.

Stierle, Karl-Heinz. *La capitale des signes: Paris et son discours.* Trans. Marianne Rocher-Jacquin. Paris: Editions de la Maison des Sciences de l'Homme, 2001.

Storey, Robert. *Pierrots on the Stage of Desire: Nineteenth Century French Literary Artists and the Comic Pantomime.* Princeton: Princeton UP, 1985.

Stovall, Floyd. *The Foreground of "Leaves of Grass."* Charlottesville: UP of Virginia, 1972.

Swinburne, Algernon Charles. "Charles Baudelaire." *The Complete Works of Algernon Charles Swinburne.* Ed. Edmund Gosse and Thomas James Wise. Vol. 13. London: Heinemann, 1926.

Swinburne, Algernon Charles. *Studies in Prose and Poetry.* London: Chatto and Windus, 1894.

Symons, Arthur. *Charles Baudelaire: A Study.* London: E. Mathews, 1920.

Tableaux vivants: Fantaisies photographiques victoriennes, 1840–1880. Paris: Edition de la Réunion des Musées nationaux, 1999.

Thézy, Marie de, ed. *Charles Marville.* Paris: Centre National de la Photographie, 1996.

Thézy, Marie de, and Roxane Debuisson, eds. *Marville Paris.* Paris: Hazan, 1994.

Thomas, M. Wynn. *The Lunar Light of Whitman's Poetry.* Cambridge: Harvard UP, 1987.

Thomas, M. Wynn. *Transatlantic Connections: Whitman US, Whitman UK.* Iowa City: U of Iowa P, 2005.

Thomas, M. Wynn. "Walt Whitman and Mannahatta–New York." *American Quarterly* 34.4 (1982) 362–78.

Thomas, M. Wynn. "Whitman's Tale of Two Cities." *American Literary History* 6.4 (1994) 633–57.

Trachtenberg, Alan. "Whitman's Lesson of the City." *Breaking Bounds: Whitman and American Cultural Studies.* Ed. Betsy Erkkila and Jay Grossman. New York: Oxford UP, 1996. 163–73.

Traubel, Horace. *With Walt Whitman in Camden.* Vol. 2. 1907. Vol. 3. 1912. New York: Rowman and Littlefield, 1961.

Trowbridge, John T. "Reminiscences of Walt Whitman." *Atlantic Monthly,* 89.2 (February 1902) 163–75.

Versluys, Kristiaan. *The Poet in the City: Chapters in the Development of Urban Poetry in Europe and the United States, 1800–1930.* Tübingen: Gunter Narr Verlag, 1987.

Veuillot, Louis. *Les odeurs de Paris.* Paris, 1867; rpt. 1911.

Warren, James Perrin. *Walt Whitman's Language Experiment.* University Park: Pennsylvania State UP, 1990.

Weil, François. *A History of New York.* Trans. J. Gladding. New York: Columbia UP, 2004.

Weimer, David. *The City as Metaphor.* New York: Random House, 1966.

Wetlaufer, Alexandra K. "Paradise Regained: The *Flâneur,* the *Badaud* and the Aesthetics of Artistic Reception in *Le poème du haschich.*" *Nineteenth Century French Studies* 24.3–4 (1996) 389–97.

Whitman, Walt. *An American Primer.* Ed. Horace Traubel. Boston: Small, Maynard, 1904.

Whitman, Walt. *The Correspondence.* Vols. 1–6. Ed. Edwin Haviland Miller. New

York: New York University P, 1961–77.

Whitman, Walt. *The Gathering of the Forces*. Ed. Cleveland Rogers and John Black. Vol. 2. New York: Putnam's, 1920.

Whitman, Walt. *Leaves of Grass*. Ed. Michael Moon. New York: Norton, 2002.

Whitman, Walt. *Leaves of Grass: Facsimile of the 1860 edition*. Ed. Roy Harvey Pearce. Ithaca: Cornell UP, 1961.

Whitman, Walt. *Leaves of Grass: The First 1855 Edition*. Ed. Malcolm Cowley. New York: Viking, 1959.

Whitman, Walt. *Notebooks and Unpublished Prose Manuscripts*. Ed. Edward F. Grier. Vol. 4, vol. 6. New York: New York University P, 1984.

Whitman, Walt. *Notes and Fragments*. Ed. Maurice R. Bucke. Ontario: A. Talbot, 1899.

Whitman, Walt. *Rivulets of Prose: Critical Essays by Walt Whitman*. Ed. Alfred H. Goldsmith and Carolyn Wells. New York: Greenberg, 1928.

Whitman, Walt. *Specimen Days and Collect*. 1883. New York: Dover, 1995.

Whitman, Walt. *The Uncollected Poetry and Prose of Walt Whitman*. Ed. Emory Holloway. Gloucester, Mass.: Peter Smith, 1972.

Whitman, Walt. *Walt Whitman's Workshop: A Collection of Unpublished Manuscripts*. Ed. Clifton J. Furness. Cambridge: Harvard UP, 1928 .

Wittgenstein, Ludwig. *Tractatus Logico-Philosophicus*. Trans. C. K. Ogden. London: Routledge & Kegan Paul, 1922.

Woodress, James. *Critical Essays on Walt Whitman*. Boston: G. K. Hall, 1983.

Wordsworth, William. *Complete Poetical Works*. London: Macmillan, 1913.

Yingling, Thomas. "Homosexuality and Utopian Discourse in American Poetry." *Breaking Bounds: Whitman and American Cultural Studies*. Ed. Betsy Erkkila and Jay Grossman. New York: Oxford UP, 1996. 135–46.

Zarobila, Charles. "Walt Whitman and the Panorama." *Walt Whitman Review* 25.1 (1979) 51–59.

Index

Agamben, Giorgio, 125n70
Algonquins, 22–23
Allegory
    and Baudelaire, 4, 69, 75–76, 97
    and Whitman, 50–51
Asselineau, Roger, 4, 70
Astor Place Theater Riot, 15
Augustine, Saint, 106–8

Balzac, Honoré de, 61, 62
Bandy, W. T., 1
Banville, Théodore de, 70, 80–81, 84
Barnum, P. T., 34–35, 37, 98
Baudelaire, Charles
    and anti-Americanism, 3, 12, 53
    and clichés, 74–77
    and dandyism, 17–18
    and dioramas, 91–93
    and Edgar Allan Poe, 2–3, 26–27,
        53, 62
    and photography, 7, 33, 94–96 (see
        also Photography)
    and trial of Les Fleurs du mal, 7
    and trompe-l'oeil, 84, 86–87, 90
    and Victor Hugo, 12, 60, 62, 86–90
    works: Artificial Edens, 52; "The
        Artist's Confiteor," 77; "Beautiful
        Dorothea," 65; "The Counterfeit
        Coin," 70, 96, 102–3; "The
        Crowds," 66, 83; "The Dog and
        the Perfume Bottle," 97; "The
        Double Bedroom," 77, 92;

"Evening Twilight," 2; "The Eyes
    of the Poor," 70, 83; Les Fleurs du
    mal, 7, 11, 14, 15, 18, 22, 49, 60,
    62–64, 69–70, 76, 79, 88–90, 92,
    94, 96, 98, 104–5, 107; "The Gal-
    lant Marksman," 89–90; "The
    Generous Gambler," 78–79; "On
    the Heroism of Modern Life" (es-
    say), 8; "A Hero's Death," 65, 82;
    Intimate Journals, 64, 74, 86; "Let
    Us Beat Up the Poor," 87; "The
    Little Old Women," 62; "Miss
    Scalpel," 63–64, 78–79, 85,
    100–101; "Morale du joujou," 90;
    "The Old Acrobat," 83–84; "The
    Old Woman's Despair," 69; "The
    Pagan School" (essay), 2, 96–97;
    "The Painter of Modern Life"
    (essay), 17, 26, 52, 64–65, 90–91;
    "Paris Dream," 45–46; "Parisian
    Scenes," 10–11, 23, 29, 40, 46;
    Petits poèmes en prose (Le Spleen de
    Paris), 11–12, 42, 58, 60, 62–64,
    69–70, 76, 79, 88–90, 92, 94, 96,
    98, 104–5; "The Projects," 93;
    "Recollection," 13, 63; "The
    Rope," 66, 69; "The Savage
    Woman and the Little Sweet-
    heart," 82, 92; "The Seven Old
    Men," 40–41, 62; "Solitude," 2,
    67; "The Stranger," 65, 78; "The
    Swan," 23, 46; "A Thoroughbred

Baudelaire, Charles (*continued*)
    Horse," 92; "To a Woman Passing
    By," 21, 47; "Which is the Real
    Benedicta?" 92; "The Widows,"
    72–73, 83, 93, 101–2; "The Win-
    dows," 74, 93
Belden, E. Porter, 38, 39
Belgium, 53, 61, 71, 98
Benjamin, Walter, 5, 9, 47, 59, 69, 89
Bentham, Jeremy, 41
Bersani, Leo, 127n15
Blin, Georges, 99, 127n15
Bourdin, Gustave, 2
Boyer, Christine M., 118n12
Brand, Dana, 28
Breton, André, 88
Broadway, 13, 16, 17, 19–22, 24–27,
    30–32, 34, 37, 40, 42–46, 48, 51,
    55, 104–5
Brooklyn, 2, 14, 19, 27, 28
Brooklyn Daily Eagle, 18, 34
Brummel, Beau (George Bryan), 7
Burke, Edmund, 39

Carjat, Étienne, 7
Carroll, Lewis, 36
Chambers, Ross, 120n52, 126n1
Champfleury (Jules Fleury-Husson),
    8, 81, 86
Clapp, Henry J., 16
Clark, Timothy James, 61
Clarke, Graham, 116n54, 116n68,
    120n53
Compagnon, Antoine, 122n32
Conrad, Peter, 20, 22, 38
Coolidge, Calvin, 1
Courbet, Gustave, 8, 91
Crary, Jonathan, 39, 42

Daguerre, Louis-Jacques-Mandé,
    91–92, 94
Dandyism, 7, 17–18
Dante, 11, 96
Daumier, Honoré, 74
Deburau, Jean-Gaspard-Baptiste, 80,
    81, 94
Deburau, Paul, 81
Delacroix, Eugène, 8, 91

Democracy
    Baudelaire's hostility to, 4–5, 18, 33
    Whitman as poet of, 3–5, 11,
        20–21, 28
Derrida, Jacques, 103
Dickens, Charles, 17
Dioramas, 36, 91–93
Douglas, Ann, 112n25
Doyle, Peter, 37
Du Camp, Maxime, 57
Dupin, Auguste, 27

Eliot, George (Mary Anne Evans), 36
Eliot, T. S., 3, 8
Emerson, Ralph Waldo, 7
Erkkila, Betsy, 112n23, 113n1,
    119n39
Étienne, Louis, 13, 15

Flaneur
    Baudelaire as, 2, 26, 41, 64–65, 67,
        78–79, 93
    in Poe's "The Man of the Crowd,"
        26–27
    and urban planning, 99–100, 109
    Whitman as, 13, 22, 24, 26–28, 37,
        54
Forrest, Edwin, 15
Foucault, Michel, 41
Fourier, Charles, 87

Gautier, Théophile, 80, 84
Gavarni, Paul (Sulpice Guillaume
    Chevalier), 74
Giedion, Siegfried, 99–100
Gilbert, Roger, 116n62
Goethe, Johann Wolfgang von, 36
Goncourt, Edmond and Jules de, 33,
    60, 61, 62, 65
Goya, Francisco de, 98
Grant, Ulysses S., 1
Guys, Constantin, 17, 26, 45, 54, 90,
    103

Haussmann, Georges-Eugène
    and Baudelaire's prose poems,
        64–65
    and centralized city planning, 16

and critics of, 61–62
and redesigning of Paris, 55–59
and time, 10–12, 99–100, 108–9
Homer, 8, 94
Houssaye, Arsène, 59, 72, 77, 129n36
Hugo, Victor, 4, 12, 60, 62, 81, 86–90

James, William, 9, 28
Journalism
and Baudelaire, 53, 67–69
and Poe, 27
and Whitman, 17–18, 30, 49, 53,
    104–5

Kafka, Franz, 83

Lacan, Jacques, 129n30
Laforgue, Jules, 8, 9, 85
Lawrence, D. H., 34
Le Vavasseur, Gustave, 91
Lévy, Michel, 70
Liszt, Franz, 66
Longfellow, Henry Wadsworth, 2
Loving, Jerome, 28

Macready, William, 15
Mallarmé, Stéphane, 98
Manet, Édouard, 66, 67
Marrinan, Richard, 129n44
Michelet, Jules, 4
Moon, Michael, 119n39
Mumford, Lewis, 16

Nadar (Gaspard-Félix Tournachon), 7
Napoleon I (Napoléon Bonaparte), 7,
    55, 91, 126n5
Napoleon III (Louis-Napoléon Bona-
    parte), 12, 55
Nerval, Gérard de, 81, 123n38,
    128n19
New York Aurora, 17, 21

O'Neill, Eugene, 55
Osgood, James, 7
Ovid, 95

Pageants
definition of, 35

in Whitman's poetry of New York,
    42–50
Panoramas
and Foucault, 41
as hybrid spectacles, 37–38
as popular entertainment, 34, 36
and Whitman's perception of New
    York, 20, 29, 37–41, 44, 47, 104
Pantomime, 34, 80–84
Parent-Duchâtelet, Alexandre,
    123n37
Pearce, Roy Harvey, 116n54
Photography
and Baudelaire's response to, 33,
    94–96
and the Goncourt brothers, 33
as metaphor of Whitman's tech-
    nique, 20
and portraits of Baudelaire and
    Whitman, 7
and Whitman's response to, 32
Plumbe, John, 32
Poe, Edgar Allan, 2, 26–27, 53, 62, 92
Poète maudit, 7
Pound, Ezra, 8
Prostitution
and Baudelaire's poem "Miss
    Scalpel," 63–64, 78–79, 85,
    100–101
as realistic topic, 7–8, 14
as urban phenomenon, 19, 49, 52
and Whitman's poem "The City
    Dead-House," 105–6
Proudhon, Joseph, 87

Realism
and Champfleury, 86
in poetry, 8–9
and popular visual entertainment,
    81, 90
Rice, Shelley, 121n5
Rimbaud, Arthur, 98
Rowdies, 13–15

Sainte-Beuve, Charles-Augustin, 1, 69,
    77, 123–24n50
Sand, George (Aurore Dupin), 4, 89
Sante, Luc, 35, 37

Sartre, Jean-Paul, 86
Spann, Edward K., 114n13
Starobinski, Jean, 75, 127n15
Stendhal (Henri Beyle), 15
Stephens, Sonya, 128n21
Stevens, Joseph, 66
Storey, Robert, 126n4
Suë, Eugène, 57, 89
Swift, Jonathan, 87
Swinburne, Algernon Charles, 14–15

Tableaux vivants, 36–37
Thiers, Adolphe, 100
Thomas, M. Wynn, 20, 28, 115n44
Trachtenberg, Alan, 20
Trompe-l'oeil, 84–90

Uchard, Mario, 70

Verlaine, Paul, 98, 123n46
Veuillot, Louis, 10
Vigny, Alfred de, 72, 77
Villon, François, 108
Violence
    in Baudelaire's prose poems, 52,
        68, 81–83, 89–90
    in *Leaves of Grass,* 51–53
    in nineteenth-century New York,
        14, 17–18, 40, 49
Virgil, 11

Waldrop, Keith, 21
Wharton, Edith, 39
Whitman, Walt
    and Francophilia, 4
    and love, 47–48
    and performance, 36–39, 43–45,
        49
    and photography, 7, 32 (*see also*
        Photography)

and realism in poetry, 8–10, 13–14
and scandal, 7–8
and transformations of New York,
    16–18
and urban violence, 14, 17–18, 40,
    49, 51–53 (*see also* Violence)
works: "Broadway," 39; "Broadway,
    1861," 21; "A Broadway
    Pageant," 42–45, 50, 51, 53–54;
    "Calamus," 30, 31, 35, 47; "The
    City Dead-House," 105–6; "City
    of Orgies," 35; "A City Walk"
    (draft of poem), 19; "Crossing
    Brooklyn Ferry," 27–30, 38; *Demo-*
    cratic Vistas, 48–50; "Drum-Taps,"
    46; "Give Me the Splendid Silent
    Sun," 19, 46–51, 53; "A Lazy
    Day," 104–5; *Leaves of Grass,* 2–5,
    7–8, 11–16, 18–23, 30–31,
    35–39, 42, 47, 49, 53, 104–5;
    "Mannahatta" (I was asking . . .),
    22–23, 38; "Of the Terrible
    Doubt of Appearances," 31; "O
    Star of France," 8; "Out of the
    Rolling Ocean the Crowd," 39;
    "Passage to India," 8; "Poetry of
    the Future" (essay), 2; "Reflec-
    tions" (draft of poem), 31–32;
    "Salut au Monde," 4; "Song of
    Myself," 23, 25, 31, 48, 51–52;
    Specimen Days, 25, 40; "Starting
    from Paumanok," 18; "To a Com-
    mon Prostitute," 8; "To a
    Stranger," 47; "A Woman Waits
    for Me," 8
Wordsworth, William, 9

Yingling, Thomas, 119n39

Zeuxis, 73
Zola, Émile, 15, 36